The

Book of

Secret Knowledge

STEVEN LOVELL FLAGG

Release – Answer

www.releaseanswer.com

New Jersey – New York

Release Answer
Po Box 3904
Newark, New Jersey

Ordering Information

For details, contact the Publisher at the address above or go to

www.Lulu.com or www.Releaseanswer.com

Printed in the United States of America

The Book of Secret Knowledge

ISBN

978-1-79488-068-9

"The Book of Secret Knowledge" is created by

Steven L. Flagg

The Founder of

Release – Answer

www.releaseanswer.com

An incredible website designed to answer any question

Note from the Author: Steven L. Flagg

Please note that this book is only based on an

opinion of life and self.

You may agree or disagree with some of the written
material in this book, and you have the right to agree or
disagree.

I'm just giving you the knowledge that I have accumulated
throughout my lifetime.

If you feel offended by any written material stated in this
book,

I apologize.

But I do have the right to express my own opinions.

This book is only an opinion.

I hope you enjoy this book, and I hope this book can be
helpful to you and your loved ones.

I love you all

NOTE:

This book is formatted differently than other books.

It is formatted to reach all levels of understanding.

Most of the book is written in a passive voice.

and

I have used prepositions at the end of sentences.

and

I have used easy words to help all readers.

CONTENTS

The
Book of
Secret Knowledge

Introduction

Life is based on worrying. We all have worried because we all are continuously trying to do more than one thing at a time. To hate something, we must worry about it. To have feelings for something, we must worry about it. To think about something, we must worry about it. To take action to do anything, we must worry about it.

Believe it or not, worrying makes things worse than it is. But we must worry about getting things done and accomplished.

Worries are only problems that need an answer. Worries are what our brains can't answer. All solved worries become solved problems and are stored in our memory banks in our minds. Without worries, there would be nothing in our memory banks to fuel our thoughts and feelings. Worrying is just not having enough information to solve what is bothering us. Once we have the answer to a given problem, we stop worrying about it.

Life is based on Lying. We are all here in this life, because we are all liars. We are here to learn how not to lie. What we all have in common is that we all can lie, and we all do lie.

To lie, we must always remember the lie. If we can't remember the lie, the lie will expire. Remembering is the key to lying.

All lies come from the mind of humans. We all have two minds, an inner and outer mind:

1. The inner mind is where the lies are created and manufactured. Lies are produced through our imagination. So, the inner mind is our Secret Society within ourselves.
2. The outer mind is where we gather information from people and things from outside of our Secret Society. Our outer mind collects information and problems that we should worry about and lie about.

If we lie, we are not telling how we feel, and we are not saying what the truth is. The truth is that everything is a lie until enough people make it the truth. Truth does not exist because no one owns the rights to the truth. So, truth is humanmade. How can anyone know all the truths when we don't even know ourselves 100%.

Life is based on what we Love. First off, love is experienced in different levels of feelings and emotions. Love eliminates worry and fear. Love motivates positive action. Love has over a billion levels of happiness and joy.

We cannot define love because there are too many happy moments associated with passion in this Universe. To feel loved, we must invite love into our lives to experience it. Love is the most potent force in the Universe.

Life is based on living. First, we all live in a circus called life. Believe it or not, we gave ourselves the rules and laws we live by. In the beginning, we had to find something for all of us to do, so we can occupy our time until we die. We needed something to do.

What we have evolved into comes from what we figured out throughout the time we spent here in this life.

Living is a timeline between Life and Death. Our job is to find ways to spend our lives before we must die. Before we die, we will have accumulated over a billion frames of memory per individual.

The question is, where do all our memories go at the end of each one of us. Do our memories go somewhere else to live, or do they die? Do our memories turn into something else, or do it just disintegrate?

That is what the end of living comes down to.

If our memories go somewhere else when it dies, it will have a chance to be judged. If our memories don't go anywhere else and get disintegrated, it would just mean that we as a Human, was just a computer, and if we are only a computer, it would mean that everything we have done doesn't mean anything.

But, if our memories get disintegrated and our Soul goes somewhere else, it would mean that all the decisions we have made while we were living would still be a part of us. So, that would mean that any situation that we encounter in the afterlife, or anywhere else that is not here, would be the same outcome of thinking. Because that is who we are.

Life is about how long we can live and how much we can learn before it is all over, and we die. But, when it is time to die, it's about who we became and what we evolve into, from what we have learned here.

So, this life is just a memory of who was here and received the chance to experience it.

We, as humans, we're able to add on and help build in this life. But, we as humans still do not know anything about this life, we live in. The sad part is that we die. We will never own this place we call Earth; all we can do is borrow it until it disintegrates. Because there are no pathways to "Forever."

So, we are all just only products of all our imaginations, and we are all just warriors of our imaginations. **We belong to each other until we die!!!**

The

Book of

Secret Knowledge

Lesson #1 Knowing Yourself

People are made from the flesh of their parents. Our body is used as a temple or vehicle to get us from one destination to another.

Body Functions:

1. The Brain is a computer center.
2. The Heart is a feeling center.
3. The Lungs are a recycling center.
4. The Kidneys and Liver are a filtering center.
5. The Veins and Arteries are the distribution center.
6. The Stomach and Intestines are the digestive centers.
7. The Eyes are the window center to see the World.
8. The Ears are the sound center for communication.
9. The Nose is the smelling center to protect the exhalation and inhalation system.

Now let's focus on the mind. But first, we need to know what Thoughts and Feelings are.

1. Thoughts are what you know, from what you see, hear, and imagine.
2. Feelings are what you feel from what you have thought or image.

Thoughts and Feelings are both created in the Brain (our internal computer).

*Thoughts are the capacity or faculty of thinking, reasoning, and imagining.

*Feelings are the general state of consciousness considered independently of sensations.

Thoughts:

1. Comes from thinking.
2. Comes from worrying.

If we want to master our thoughts, we must create another file in our Brain, and call it "Life 2."

1. Our regular everyday thinking will be the file, "Life 1."
2. Now start another file and name the new file. "Life 2."

Life 1, we will always have it because we have created it from birth to the present time.

Life 2 will allow us to think of more things; it's like giving ourselves an extra bedroom to think in. Life 2 will let us escape the World.

Don't worry so much about Life 1; we already have enough information in that file; for now, start focusing on Life 2; it will serve as an extra brain. Think of it as if you must start learning how to write with your other hand for a while.

Feelings:

1. Sad
2. Annoyed
3. Worried
4. Happy
5. Scared
6. Nervous
7. Angry
8. Greedy
9. Excited
10. Frustrated
11. Upset
12. Surprised
13. Intense
14. Tired
15. Embarrassed
16. Disappointed
17. Confused
18. Impatient
19. Curious
20. Proud

All these feelings come from our thoughts. People say that the mind is from the Brain, but that is "bullshit"! However, if we believe that to be true, we will give our brains more power over ourselves.

The mind is who we are. The mind is not a body part nor a place in the Brain. The mind can adjust to any situation at any giving time, even if the body is healthy or sick. Whatever body we receive at our final birth, the mind will adapt to it immediately.

Brain Exercise:

1. Questions are created for curious people.
2. Answers came from things that seem impossible to solve.
3. Problems are everything that is skeptical.
4. Opinions are just a guess.
5. The proof is just a solution to a problem.
6. A Test will measure what we know.
7. Methods are created experiments.
8. Results come from change.
9. Important are things we are attracted to.
10. Different is something of another kind.
11. Search, and Discover is Research.
12. Facts are clues to the truth.
13. Trying is looking for what we need.
14. Growing is when things get better.
15. Probably is accepting things for what we think it is until we find the truth about it.

Questions require information that is already available.

Answers are the outcomes of solving tough questions.

Lesson #2 Systems

All Living things are Systems. A System depends on its parts. When all the elements of a system are working correctly, the system runs smoothly, just the way it should. Every piece has a role in keeping the system working.

Systems come in all shapes and sizes. Some systems are parts of other networks. If you remove a part of a system, the system will not work correctly or may not ever work again.

Systems are a set of detailed methods, procedures, rules, laws, and routines created to carry out specific goals or to solve various problems.

Each element of a system influences each part (directly or indirectly).

All systems have inputs, outputs, and feedback mechanisms.

Systems stop functioning when an element is removed or change significantly.

There are eight systems that we need in life:

1. **Life System:** A system of surviving until we die.
2. **Government system:** A system to establish order, providing security, and accomplishing shared goals.
3. **School system:** is a system of learning.
4. **Health system:** is a network of people, institutions, and resources that delivers health-related services to meet the needs of a target population.
5. **Money system:** is a system that drives the economy through transactions of trading and buying of goods, services, and financial assets.
6. **Food system:** A system that provides us with key nutrients to keep us healthy and happy, it starts from agriculture, then it goes to food processing manufacturers, then to retail, then to the people.
7. **Home system:** is a system to build shelters out of material, to give shelter for a dwelling place for human beings.
8. **Clothing system:** is a system to cover ourselves with animal skin and other materials to hide our body parts and to protect us from cold.

Lesson #3 Change

Change = it changes things that once were some other way of operating.

The change will set things into motion, and motion forces things to change.

Motion = is anything that moves or makes energy.

Energy = sound, light, heat.

Energy is a source that absorbs, reflects, and dissolves; it brings forth change.

These are the single-handed weapons of change.

Life is defined by change. Every day the world change.

Things that makes us change:

1. Loss
2. Struggles
3. Hurt
4. Mistakes
5. Lies
6. Beliefs
7. Love
8. Hatc
9. Progress
10. Money
11. Opinions
12. Thoughts

"You never change your life until you step out of your comfort zone; change begins at the end of your comfort zone."

Lesson #4 Options

There are options in life. But we only choose a few shortcuts that work the best for our lives, until they don't work anymore, then we go out of the way to find other options.

We get our options from what we see or hear. We give away most of our lives to options.

There's always another option, so don't just limit yourself to only the ones you know.

Example:

1. Money gives us more options.
2. Sometimes crying or laughing are the only options available.
3. Sometimes quitting is the only option.

Most of the World's problems are caused by people who choose the wrong options.

Please remember: There's always another option, never limit yourself to only the options you know.

If you must choose in a small limit of time, remember the options you have on the table but quickly think of more options before you give into a determined choice.

Options give you:

1. Opportunities
2. Possibilities

With options, we can design our desires; without options, we are at the mercy of others.

Without options, our choices are limited, and we must accept what we are given.

Options are about taking risks, and our challenges need options.

When something happens, we need options. The more options we have, the less stress we will have.

We use options to accept, avoid, and change.

With Options we can only:
1. Do nothing
2. Do better
3. Do worse

Choosing options are the only journey to follow in life.

Life with options is freedom of living life the way we choose to.

Lesson #5 Mistakes

All mistakes have a reason behind it, like math; it just never equals up to what it was intended to be.

You can fix a mistake by adding something else with it or by subtracting something from it.

A mistake is a wrong calculation that needs direction, and the route is finding out the answer from someone who made that same mistake before and corrected it.

Mistakes are part of the learning process; it is one of the elements of learning.

It is essential to make mistakes in the learning process.

Mistakes are used as a platform to teach others what to watch out for.

Mistakes are needed for success.

Mistakes are proof that we are trying.

Mistakes show us what needs improvement.

Mistakes become an experience.

Mistakes:

1. Comes from accidents
2. Wrong choices
3. Wrong Information
4. Bad judgment
5. Carelessness
6. Misunderstanding
7. Misconceptions
8. Poor reasoning
9. Insufficient Knowledge
10. Miscalculation

Without mistakes, we will not know what we must work on. Every mistake gives us useful information about our lives.

When we make a mistake and do the wrong thing, we must figure out what we did wrong and make an exit plan. The exit plan is what makes us a better person.

So, a mistake = a miss take, we must redo it and do it right.

Lesson #6 Judgement

People are judged all the time unfairly. We all are judged daily. We may be judged by our appearance, the way we talk, or just by the material items we own. People's first impressions mean a lot, but the way you view them should not be based on only appearance. Before you assess the kind of person you think someone is, you should stop and get to know them first.
Everyone has their tastes, styles, and opinions. Some people choose to wear clothing that is "in style," while others prefer to wear clothing that suits their taste.

Judging others sometimes gives people a sense of prestige because demeaning others can create a false sense of security and identity. When it comes down to it, people are different. No two people are entirely alike. We need to accept these differences and stop judging people. It is hurtful to them and makes the people ridiculing them look bad.

People are judged unfairly because of where they came from, what they do for a living, how much money they make, what color or sex they are, what clothes they wear or cars they drive, right down to how they spend their free time.

Every person in the World passes some type of judgment on a person before speaking to them; they do that because they are prejudice. They judge people for the way they look or act, but they don't really know the person, so they automatically put them in a particular group, and that is how they will always remember that person.

In life, we will always judge others, and we will always be judged.

Universal Judgements:

1. Good & Bad
2. Right & Wrong
3. Happy & Sad
4. Truth & Lie
5. Real & Fake

We must judge everything in life to process our thinking.

Lesson #7 Arguing

Arguing is explaining why we are right. Arguing is trying to convince other people to believe things they don't want to consider. Arguing is trying to make other people think something they don't want to remember.

An argument is a series of statements intended to determine the degree of truth of another statement. Arguments attempt to show that something was, is, will be, or should be. An argument is a set of ideas put together to support a point. It is a weapon to protect our beliefs and self-interests.

In everyday life, we often use the word argument to mean a verbal dispute or disagreement.

Arguing is a system to win.

Arguing is used in:

1. Law
2. Medical
3. Politics
4. Religion
5. Business
6. Science
7. Society

In an argument, either we are trying to explain something true, or we are trying to explain something that we only have an opinion of. Most of the time people argue over opinion. And most of the time, people will not support our opinion.

Arguments are head-on confrontations. Arguments create war. Arguing is about who is right and who is wrong. Everyone involved in the debate is only trying to challenge each other ideas.

Psychology suggests that arguments are only an appeal to the reasoning of wishful thinking.

To win an argument, we must use facts and evidence to support our case, to shut the other person down. If you only speak on matters that you know, you will always win.

So, remember in an argument, the other person is out to defeat you.

Lesson #8 Street Smart

Wisdom = the study of lies & truth.

Wisdom is a skill set that weighs your:

1. Experience
2. Knowledge
3. Good Judgment

When it is time to decide.

Wisdom is based on book smart related to the right situations and outcomes.

Street Smart = getting out of trouble.

Street Smart is a safety skill designed to:

1. Keep us aware of our surroundings
2. Help us deal with difficulties
3. Keep us away from bad situations

There are six rules to being Street Smart:

1. Don't trust anyone
2. Every day is an opportunity that we don't get back
3. Every move we make must be a power move
4. Don't believe everything you read
5. Study people actions
6. Think ahead of everyone you encounter

Dealing with people:

1. Don't think about what they are saying to you 100%, think more about what they are trying to get out of you or from you.
2. People want you to fulfill their "purpose."
3. You must think three steps ahead of everyone that you communicate with.

Example: If someone is talking to you, listen to what they say, then think what they will do or say in the next three times you would hear from them again. So, fuck what they are saying, just think about what they want from you.

You must think beyond every communication.

REMEMBER this, 'Everybody wants you to buy their story", and "Everybody wants to be in a secret." People will not always get what they want, so they are always starving for want they want.

Realistically, you and I are starving for what we can't get also.

So, in a nutshell, everyone we encounter wants us to be their excuse for what they do, (they make a way to blame us).

The Science of Street Smart:

Street Smart is an instinct that helps us fulfill our purpose, and it helps us find our highest "Self."

Street Smart Vs. Book Smart

1. Book Smart contains the best lies with the most truth, and books are designed to cut off our higher brain actives.

    Book Smart = is what you read.

2. Street Smart builds our common sense, it teaches us how things work without applying education methods.

    Street Smart = What you see.

You may want to say, what about school:

School = A system of thoughts, beliefs, human findings, and theories.

Most of our intelligence is gained outside of school in the real world.

Street Smart:

Street Smart means you've put yourself at risk and have survived.

Street Smart means that you've learned how to take what has happened to you (good or bad) and improved from it.

Street Smart is knowing when people are trying to fuck you over.

Street Smart is reading people's intentions and determining what is not bullshit.

Street Smart is thinking more then you speak and knowing more then you say.

The Religion of Street Smart:

Don't think about what you already know; just watch how people get out of problems and record it to your memory bank.

You must understand every kind of person and race to know all the current things that are happening in the streets.

Two Secrets:

1. You cannot kill the truth; you can only hide it.
2. Success is a warm place to hide.

What's going on in the urban streets.

Knowing what is going on in the urban streets is just like knowing the stock market. The stock market goes up and down, the urban streets go up and down also. The stock market closes at the end of the day, but urban the streets never close.

You must pay very careful attention to the way things work, to develop a way to channel all the money to you.

When you know how people think and feel, you will know what to do and how to help them. Having access to people's thoughts will give you a better idea of how people think. Ask for advice and opinions to tap into people's knowledge.

Book Smart is like reading musical notes.

Street Smart is like playing music by ear.

Street Smart is something you don't learn in school; it is the ability to read people better than most other people.

Street Smart is paying attention to details that tell you what is going on.

Street Smart is knowing what you don't know and knowing what you must know.

Street Smart is what turns desires into results.

Street Smart means to follow your instincts and to listen to your gut and to try not to overthink things.

Street Smart is the awareness of how to survive in an often-bad urban environment.

Learn people's values, beliefs, and temptations to be a perfect street-smart person.

Example: If someone says to you: "I'm going, to be honest with you," Ask them what else haven't they been honest with you about and wait for their answer.

Street Smart:

Intelligence gained outside of school. Just as useful as book smarts, and in many cases, more so. It can be divided into four categories.

1. Getting Along with Others- Knowing which questions to ask and not asking too many, being polite and friendly, but also being assertive.

2. Common Sense- Knowing who you can trust, which areas in town are good and which are bad, etc.

3. Self-defense-Knowing how to fight and fend off an attacker, especially if you are small.

4. BS-detection-Knowing when people are trying to fuck you over, reading their intentions, and knowing that most corporate advertisements are complete bullshit.

Street Smart Glossary:

Angry = Out of options

Afraid = Fear

Sad = Lost

Hate = Disbelief

Rejection = Left out

Disgust = Not being a part of what you like.

Upset = Things is not going your way.

Guilt = Wish you never did what you have done.

Envy = You want what the other person has.

Calmness = You got over, what you encountered.

Surprise = Didn't believe in something, until it was proven.

Shy = Scared to say what is on your mind.

Cruelty = Enjoy hurting people if it doesn't hurt you.

Devotion = Never telling on people when they do something wrong.

Courage = Standing up for you and your family.

Kind = Caring and hoping for attention or a reward.

Love = Wanting

Happy = Feeling no sad now.

Wisdom = Knowing all the lies of a talked-about subject.

Lesson #9 Life

Life is about taking chances:

1. The right to choose
2. Options
3. Possibilities
4. Opportunities
5. Selections
6. Discoveries
7. Risk
8. Prediction
9. Adventure
10. Hope

Life choices bring:

1. Meeting others
2. Understanding
3. Accidents
4. Necessity
5. Happenings
6. Want
7. Control
8. Desires
9. Imagination
10. Hazards

Life brings forth changes:

1. Belief
2. Being
3. Going
4. Becoming

Life revolves around feelings of:

1. Love
2. Hate
3. Pain
4. Fear
5. Hurt

Feelings = are what is more relevant to everyone.

Each person's feelings are different from all others. The most common feelings are "good and bad." The best feelings are "love and pain."

What hurts us is our feelings. We can only have compassion for the things we can see, hear, and touch.

Love and hate are the top feelings that change lives.

But fear is the most powerful feeling of all.

Life is about who can lie to you the best.

Right and Wrong / Truth and Lie, all need a reason to be.

Everything is a lie until enough people decided to make it the truth. (a fact)

A lie is when you hold back the truth.

Everyone has their version of right and wrong.

Anyone can lie about anything they want to.

Lies are what each of us has in common.

Will Life ever be a part of:

1. Death
2. Forever

All we know is that life will always blast a hole into today to get to tomorrow until something blasts a hole into "LIFE."

Lesson #10 Who we are (Part #1)

We were given this life because we are strong enough to live it.

We were created to create.

We are who we are.

No one can make us be who we are not:

1. No person
2. No source or force
3. No spirit or religion

Unless we give up our rights.

How can anything change us? It can't, because any chance we get, we will only go back to who we are?

We will always be who we are, even in:

1. The public
2. School
3. Home
4. At work
5. Church
6. Even in heaven.

The very moments that challenge us the most will determine who we are going to be. Who we are, depends on our definition of self and happiness?

There is always something to threaten our happiness, and that feeling of threat is where our souls' dwell.

No matter what your happiness is, you will always lose it from time to time, to find it back, to create new happiness.

1. People take our Happiness.
2. Mistakes take our happiness.
3. New joy takes our current happiness.

So, live your life to the fullest because you never know when it will end.

Lesson #11 Who we are (Part #2)

We are where we are today because of the achievements of over ten billion human minds in our lifetime. Our experiences are not our own, they are forced on us to handle it ourselves. We are all complicated and part of something bigger than ourselves.

We have created our own systems. All problems are already solved, and the people who have the answers will not share it. There are systems for all resources.

There are secret systems of knowledge. There are also systems for our minds, such as letters make words, words make sentences, sentences make paragraphs, paragraphs make stories, stories make ideas, ideas make thoughts, thoughts control the mind.

Question??? "Do words and definitions make us smart, or do it limit us to only things we need to know?

Systems:

We choose what systems and situations to involve ourselves in.

Universal Control Systems:

1. Religion – Controls good and bad.
2. Time – Controls sense of order, sequence, movement. (without time, we couldn't count, counting takes time)
3. Life - Controls the earth.
4. Water and Food – Controls Life.
5. Eyes – Controls what we see.
6. Ears – Controls what we hear.
7. Faith – Controls our hope.

Faith is passing our responsibility to a higher power, being, or substance. We use faith because we are too lazy to work out our problems. The truth is that faith is an old feeling. What takes the place of the prehistoric "Faith" is just "being happy."

Being ourselves is a full-time job. There is always something to work on in our lives. Everything we do is an extra step for us. We all need a reason to do the things we do. Our minds always keep our company, even when we are sleep. Our feelings are born only from our thoughts.

Whenever we explain something to others, we are teaching them. So, with that in mind, "Everyone is technically stupid." We don't know if there is life after death. We must convince ourselves many times during each day that everything will be alright. We cannot see the World clearly for what it is. So, stupid is only a delay in being smart. Remember This: Life will only happen for you, only once, so, just do your best until you learn better, then do better.

Lesson #12 Universal Truth

The Truth today is very different from the truth 1000 years ago. Because reality today is based on all the facts that we have made for ourselves up to date. One thousand years ago, we had to cut through so many lies to determine the truth. But today. Most lies are figured out. So, truth and lies are both humanmade. We will never experience the full meaning of truth until all lies die.

Everybody must uphold what they believe to be true in their lives.

Question??? Is truth a rule, or is it an opinion?

To debate, if the truth is a rule or an opinion, you must debate an issue from both sides.

Example:

If you believe that there are two sides to a story, and you must choose a side, and you think that one side is truth (a rule), then the other side is just an opinion.

Guess what. When you choose a side, you are deciding that there is only one right side.

Truth – the objective is to make one idea win and another lose. The outcome is to see what's there as honestly and accurately as you can. Truth = facts and evidence.

Truth frees you from faith, fear, and intimidation. You cannot form beliefs of truth without evidence.

Different religions separate the truth. The truth is a way of searching for the strategy to be right. The truth was invented to stop the lies. Both truth and lies have the same power and control because we gave truth the same power as lies.

Now Let's talk about the truth:

First, you must know that every human being that was on Earth before us has made us all live a certain way. They learned how to live, but they didn't know what life was. Life had no meaning to it at that time. So, they created religion to control the human mind; then, they became prisoners to religion. Later religion became the primary source of life. Religion was designed to find one moment of joy somewhere, whereas we would not have to worry so much about death.

As we developed more as a human being, we started communicating and setting names to objects, events, people, and things. Once an object and event were named, it became the truth or law of it, then that's how truth began.

Today truth equals Law.

The truth of humans = came from the first individuals on Earth, based on their experiences and beliefs.

Universal Truth:

1. There is a sun, moon, stars, trees, water, and dirt
2. There are clouds, wind, rain, snow
3. It takes a woman about nine months to deliver a baby
4. All humans will live and die
5. All humans need a body to survive
6. There are objects and minerals on Earth
7. There are other animals on Earth besides human
8. Human need food and water to survive
9. Humans need sleep to help produce a healthy body.
10. All humans are designed to grow old

All other truths are humanmade.

Example: Let's say there is an object that is "blue," but you believe it to be green, and everybody around you tells you it is "blue." Would "blue" be true and green be false? The truth is that someone named the color "blue, so you would have to go back in history to find out who invented the name of the color "blue." Blue is only a name, not a fact, so it is humanmade.

Humans make rules, and rules create the truth. Right and wrong both came from the laws of honesty.

Example: Let's say an individual puts a gold watch (that is not his) in his pocket, which was on a coffee table in someone else's home, and there were ten other people around, looking for it.

The individual who put the watch in his pocket would be the only person who knows that the watch is in his pocket. So, no one else will see the truth until that individual reveals that he has taken the watch.

Or if maybe someone saw him take the watch, or at some point, it drops out of his pocket.

So, the truth belongs to individuals who know what each truth is made of. All truths are made from facts.

If we don't know what the truth is made of, we will never know the "Truth."

We don't have reference to the truth of how humanity was created. The only way to know the truth for ourselves, we would have to meet the Creator itself.

Truth is a map of how things should be.

Scientific truth = What things are

Human truth = is what's right for you and society

Religion truth = How you should act

Truth is only a point of view. Truth is a temporary belief of knowing something in a moment until it advances or changes.

Theory of Truth:

The truth must be discovered. After it is located, the truth becomes the final answer.

Truth is the best challenge of life, because all facts were well researched. A claim well supports all truths.

A statement is true when it says what is "IS" or what it is not 'IS NOT."

So, truth doesn't matter anymore, what matters is what you need the facts for.

Today Truth:

The 1800's to 1900's truth is dead. Truth is in trouble every day these days. Society no longer cares about truth; now, it is up to the people to decide what is right and wrong. Today people sell the truth. In, Religion, Books, YouTube, Facebook, Twitter, Internet.

All we can get out of the truth is that people will support it.

Either you tell the truth like it is, or it is a "Lie." Whatever "IS" is true, it's not what anyone thinks it is. Life is what it is, and we developed truth to understand it. We choose what to believe in. Everyone cannot see everything in life, so we have learned from each other to see the things we were unable to see. As a result, people have lied to us, forcing us to find the truth for ourselves. If we don't know the truth for ourselves, all we could do is only trust in other people.

The Truth is that Human life is a mystery, and the Creator is outside of what we know.

Lesson #13 How to get out of Problems

Problems come from the things we can't figure out.

Problems are just a warning of missing information.

Problems become problems when we don't have enough information to solve them.

When the heart hurts, it tells us that there is a problem with us, either physically or mentally.

Problem Solutions:

1. If you do the opposite of the problem, it will set you free 75% of the time.

Example:

a) Up vs. Down
b) Open vs. Close
c) Near vs. Far

We learn this in school, but, no one pays attention.

2. You can go to people and experts who know the solution to your problem.

Example:

a) If you have health problems, go to the "Doctor."
b) If you have a toothache, go to the "Dentist."
c) If you have a question that you can't answer, go to www.releaseanswer.com

Don't waste your time on a problem that has an answer to it already, just located the answer.

All answers come from solved problems.   **"Memory"**

Release – Answer

www.releaseanswer.com

Lesson #14 The Energy of Problems

Energy:

It takes energy to love and hate.

It takes energy to be happy, sad, mad, strong, and weak.

It takes energy to have stress, fear, sympathy, concern, passion, remorse, pride, sorrow, and desire.

Energy brings emotions to life; it also learns from our experiences.

Energy reacts to emotions and imagination.

1. Reactions = Motion
2. Energy and Motion = Emotion

Emotion defines the real feeling of a feeling.

From emotions comes **"Mental Accidents"** such as:

1. Crying
2. Bleeding
3. Sweating

Which is all created by water

Each person has a unique emotion pattern.

Problems:

Everybody has their own set of challenges.

The first problem is the fact that we didn't create ourselves, so we don't know what to do with ourselves, either we do things to ourselves or for ourselves.

Questions:

1. What are we?
2. What is this World?
3. Where do we come from?
4. How did we get here?
5. Where are we going?

These are all unanswered questions.

The biggest question is, "Who manufactured us."

The truth is that we are all in this World like "Toys."

So, what is the purpose of our lives, and why are we here:

1. Who programmed us?
2. Did we come with instructions?

No one knows the answer, "Now, where does truth fit in."

The truth is that we all are losing and sacrificing our lives, running after:

1. Money
2. Sex
3. Power

We involve our lives into stupid things, which is allowing life to slip out of our own hands and into death. We will realize it only at the time of death.

What we have created by ourselves:

1. We have found better ways of existing for ourselves.
2. We have figured out the nature of being alive.
3. We have discovered how to adapt to what earth is made of.

What the earth is made of became our first problem to solve.

That problem gave us "awareness." Then other issues became a challenge for us.

We then learned to hide our problems.

Our main problem today is that we are always trying to figure out what each person is thinking.

The truth is that we will not reveal what we have inside us until we choose to and believe it or not; the Creator is the same way.

So, the energy of problems creates a way to help and teach disadvantaged people to become advantage people to help others with issues.

Lesson #15 Information

First, we can do anything we want in our minds. In our minds, every day, we get rid of information to make room for new information.

We must sleep to organize our days' information; Sleep takes away 36% of our lives. By the year 2045, sleep will be diagnosed as an "Illness."

Information makes us who we are.

Information becomes energy, and it travels through our bodies.

Everything in the Universe is information. Information got us to where we are now. We cannot think without information.

Example:

If someone asks you a question that requires an answer, it all boils down to

1. Do you think you know the answer? (or)
2. Do you know the answer?

If you think you know the answer, it means you don't know if you have the correct information to answer it correctly. But, if you know the answer, it means you have the accurate information available to answer it correctly.

Information changes the way we think.

Information is all around us; it is designed for us to hand it down to our next generation.

Information consists of:

1. Truth
2. Lies

To determine if the information is true or false, we must know:

1. Truth is above all differences.
2. Truth is the most powerful weapon in the World.

However, sadly, we live what we are told; either we believe what we are told, or we don't believe what we are told.

Belief:

With belief, we give things a purpose, so we can have something to believe in.

Where we are in life is based on what we believe.

Belief System:

1. Belief is an idea that we hold to be true.
2. Belief judges' principles to be true.
3. Belief is part of a network of other beliefs.
4. A lot of different beliefs secures opinions.
5. Belief is a library of what you believe to be true in your brain.
6. Belief is secondhand information.

Belief involves emotions of right and wrong.

Right and wrong = "good and bad." Good and bad become energies.

Energy:

All energies have a feeling and thought attached to it.

1. Feelings – tells us what supports our survival and what subtracts from our survival.
2. Thoughts – tells us what is good about the feeling and what is bad about the feeling.

We need three things to create a feeling:

1. Belief
2. Information
3. Truth or false

We need three things to create a thought:

1. Belief
2. Information
3. Imagination

We need three things to create belief:

1. Truth or False
2. Information
3. Want

Today's Information:

Today our lives are based on what we feel.

We have learned to put bad situations behind us.

Today, we are taking more chances with our lives, more than ever, even when we know what the consequences are.

Today everything is appreciated by something else, which means we are being programmed to be liked by as many people as possible.

Reference:

1. Facebook
2. Twitter
3. Facebook
4. Google
5. YouTube
6. Social Media

Today, everyone is addicted to likes on social media. They give up information, personal information, and secret information to be liked.

Today, the internet is our second life.

The internet is designed to allow one person to influence another person.

The internet allows us to transport information by:

1. Drawings of pictures
2. Videos
3. Emails
4. Messages
5. Contacts
6. Audio

The function of the internet is to:

1. Collect Information
2. Process Information
3. Store Information

Information systems have made life very easy for all individuals, Society, Corporations, Religious Organizations, Governmental Agencies, and Countries.

So, it would be wise to gather all the information you need from the internet.

Lesson #16 Understanding People

Our goal is to create and communicate better.

We are all in a system that we have created for ourselves.

This system we call life is just an institution and everything we do is within it.

In this institution, we call life; we are programmed to give meaning to all the things we can see and hear.

We are programmed from school. School programs our brain. School is just a learned memory. Believe it or not, everything we know was programmed in us.

So, in other words, we must go to school to be a part of the System.

Vision:

Every day, everyone lends their vision (thoughts) to others. We will have to agree or disagree with their visions. The insights give us options to learn more than what we currently know. The concepts either become an opportunity or a problem. Either way, visions become "growth," and there will always be consequences in growth.

63

Example:

When you give to others at the degree that you must sacrifice yourself, you will eventually make the other person a thief.

Because they would be stealing from you what you need for yourself. However, they would not be aware of it.

There are growth and declines in all matters and situations.

Every moment we must choose from the thoughts we have, which makes us an observer of our thoughts.

There are things about us that we may never see:

1. Our real self always knows the truth about us.
2. Our highest need is love and belonging to something.
3. We have followed the true core of something all our lives.
4. We don't know what good is until we have experienced it for ourselves.
5. We are all linked to something that never sleeps.
6. Our minds are designed from the way we were raised as children.
7. Money changes our outcomes.

Lesson #17 Super Self

Your Super Self is a higher or better part, version, or aspect of yourself.

Your Super Self is the inner person in you that you must negotiate with each day.

Your Super Self job is to learn from experiences to obtain the facts of life.

Your Super Self is not an entity separate from you; it is very much a part of you.

Your Super Self is the highest aspect of you that can be attained and held in the physical body.

Your Super Self is the part of you that knows, sees, and understands at the highest level possible.

Your Super Self is the real you; it is so much more than the physical form of you.

Your Super Self knows everything about you, it also guards your secrets and desires.

Your Super Self wants you to figure out things for yourself.

Connecting with your Super Self:

When you are in tune with your Super Self:

1. You start to pay attention to your thoughts.
2. You start to watch your thoughts and notice how it is affecting you.
3. You start to watch how you feel.
4. You start hearing with your "eyes."
5. You start seeing with your "ears."

In other words, you must connect within to find the answers you need.

You must think in terms of:

1. Energy
2. Vibration
3. Frequency

Energy = Eating the right foods to keep your body healthy. Good food is medicine for your body.

When your Vibration and Frequency is low, you will attract:

1. Depression
2. Sadness
3. Fear
4. Anxiety

So, you must be conscious of what you are feeding your Mind and Body.

Lesson #18 Better Yourself

Keys to better yourself to Success:

1. Tell people how to behave in your life.
2. Make things and people honor you.
3. Demand what you want.
4. What people think about you shouldn't be any of your business.

Bettering yourself improves your quality of life and gives you something to work towards.

There are so many things in your life that you want to get better at, but for some reason, you keep falling short of your expectations.

The problem is that we tend to try to better ourselves all at once rather than concentrate on one important thing at a time, allowing ourselves to build up momentum over months and years.

The best way to better yourself is to learn where your sense of self-worth comes from.

Self-Worth:

Self-worth is an internal state of being that comes from self-understanding, self-love, and self-acceptance.

To have a high level of self-worth means having a favorable opinion or estimate of yourself.

To have a high level of self-worth always means accepting yourself wholeheartedly.

Self:

1. The knowing of self = you see your feelings.
2. Not lying to yourself = tells you how you feel.
3. Forgiving yourself, right away when you fail = will make your bad feelings disappear.

Worth:

1. A quantity of something of a specified value:

Self-Worth is the process of recognizing your true self and finding what you are worth.

To better yourself, you must look around for things that bother you and see if you can fix it.

Remember, your job is to be the best yourself you can be because it is always all about you.

Lesson #19 Being Satisfied

Human Psychology:

The more we expect, the more we suffer when we don't receive what we expect.

The more we get, the more we expect, and when we don't receive, the more we suffer.

If being satisfied is a destination you are waiting to arrive at, then you could be in for a long ride. Being satisfied is different for everybody, or it is better to say that every person has his level of being satisfied. Being satisfied doesn't happen out of anywhere – it must be worked on; it must be produced, created, discovered, and built from the ground up.

Being satisfied has many different definitions for many different people and being satisfied changes under certain circumstances. For many people, being satisfied could be having money and power, meanwhile for another person, being satisfied could be being healthy and having certain things in their life in a good position.

Being satisfied is our goal per our being.

The truth is that people are never satisfied with what they have; they always want something more or something different. They always focus on the things they don't have.

They focus on thoughts of:

1. I don't have enough.
2. I want and need something else.
3. I need something better.
4. I want that.

The truth is that we are all greedy, wanting more than what we already have.

Greed:

Greed is not a bad thing; it is good! Greed has been the primary motivating factor in every significant historical, scientific, social, and economic event so far. Without greed, our economy would fail overnight. Without greed, there would be no religion. Without greed, governments would cease to exist. Without greed, all the currencies in the world wouldn't be worth anything at all. It is the greed of the worker, striving to earn more money, which drives our country and the world forward.

So, unfortunately, being satisfied means you are not doing anything productive in your Life.

"Not being satisfied is imagining and dreaming of a better you." So, choose wisely if you would like to be satisfied or not, the choice is yours.

Lesson #20 The Movement of Thought

Thinking:

1. Thinking – is the time between the question and answer.
2. Thinking – is searching.
3. Thinking – is the process of understanding what we see and hear.
4. Thinking – is uncomfortable, because it takes plenty of effort.

When we say, "I don't know," it means, we have stop thinking and searching for an answer.

The Thought System:

1. Who = Whom I'm thinking about?
2. What = What I'm thinking about?
3. When = When did it happen?
4. Where = Where did it happen?
5. How = How did it happen?
6. Which = Which things are involved?
7. Why = Why did it happen?
8. Would = What would make it better?
9. Could = Could this be true?
10. Should = Should it be like this?
11. Will = What will I do?

These are some of the questions that your mind must answer to be able to think about something.

Think of a thought as an investigation tool.

Thinking has a timeline. In this timeline, the brain-computer gathers information from the library that you have created from learning the things you know and the things you learned in school.

Each thought makes a "Change," and only a few thoughts become reality.

Thoughts can correct mistakes and make more mistakes.

Some thoughts are just predictions that fade out or breaks down in the thought process while you are creating thoughts.

Each thought has an emotion attached to it; either it will be negative or positive.

All our thoughts come from what we believe and what we believe determines what we make true.

60% of our thought system is what we have learned in school. School is a system that we all have within us.

What are we supposed to do?

There are things that we as people "Supposed to do," but we have a choice of:

1. Are we going to continue to do what we supposed to do?
2. Are we going to do what we not supposed to do?

Well, if we decide to not continue to do what we supposed to do, it will bring forth "Change."

"Suppose to do" – is not a thing people are doing these days. People are doing more of the "Not supposed to do" because they can do whatever they want to do.

Example:

People supposed to go to the bathroom to urinate, but some people urinate in the street and alongside buildings.

We can sit here all day and write down all the things people are not supposed to do.

We are programmed that, if we don't do what we supposed to do we will:

1. Go to hell
2. Go to jail
3. Go to bed
4. Be fired
5. Be suspended
6. Be killed
7. Be Injured

Humans have come a long way. In the beginning, we didn't know anything about ourselves nor this planet and its resources.

Now we have established Government, Religion, Health Care, Jobs, Transportation, Schools, Banks, Supermarkets, etc.

We did all of this with the movement of our thoughts.

Lesson #21 Energy of Money

We are currently living in a society in which money has become the objective of everything we can think of. Money has become more important than human life.

The truth is that we invented money to share our goods and services with others.

Our goods and services circulate through the flow of money.

Money is the System of Life:

We were programmed to love money at a young age. Today we can't live without money.

1. Money is an instrument that satisfies our desires.
2. Money is an instrument that pays for our debts.
3. Money is the key element that stands in between us and getting our needs met.

Today, money determines how we live our lives. We have traded our lives in for cash.

Money is getting more potent than Planet Earth. We value money more than life itself.

Today, we use money in every transaction we conduct. It is challenging to sustain without money, as it is the necessity of living.

History of Money:

In the beginning, money was just an idea to help circulate goods and services. Then it became an IOU receipt or claim check that we could use later to get other goods and services. Then we learned how to have people borrow the IOU receipts (money) without exchanging goods or services, but for a fee.

Money was created as a note for the exchange of goods and services. We invented money to share our goods and services with others. Our wants and needs for the goods and services are what keeps the money circulating.

We used the money to buy goods and services, as well as received money for our products and services. The money that we received for our goods and service were used to buy what we needed and wanted. Money was also deposited in banks for a fee. The banks then used 90% of our deposited cash for people that need to borrow money.

Then the Banks let us borrow the IOU receipts (money) to buy things that we want and need, in which we cannot afford to pay right away for an interest fee, which will put us in debt (owing the borrowed amount plus the interest fee) to the banks. Banks create money from deposits we make and make money from our debts. If there is no deposits and loans, there will be no more money, and if all debts were to be paid off, it would leave our society with no money at all.

We are living in the system of Money.

Today, money is how we live life.

Today, money has taken on the form of a GOD.

People will:

1. Fight for it
2. Kill for it
3. Die for it

Money has power over people.

Money also has the power to bring people together as well as tear them apart.

We are all in prison with money because money makes our lives a service.

Money makes us:

1. Work for it
2. Spend it
3. Save it
4. Hold it
5. Think about it

Money started from trading to paper to plastic cards to internet terminals.

Today, money flows through computers at incredible speeds.

The truth is that we need money to survive, and in our society, money is everything.

Today, people want and need money more than anything.

All we can do is keep buying money for ourselves by:

1. Working
2. Selling our goods and services.
3. Borrowing

It is what it is because, we all collectively agreed to make money what it is, and in this life, everything is for sale.

Release – Answer

www.releaseanswer.com

Lesson #22 Society Vs. Religion

Life – is the one thing that unifies all of us. It's a life story that will be told to the generations to come.

Life – is just a bunch of stories; each person that lives to be old has three stories:

1. When they were a baby until an adult.
2. When they were an adult to old.
3. When they were old to death.

Life – is like a wave; we are all riding; we just become born and start riding life immediately.

Life is a craving for information.

Life – is Developing, Learning, Experiencing.

1. Developing – is growing and evolving.
2. Learning – is experiencing and remembering.
3. Experiencing – encountering and undergoing something.

In life, there are Challenges, Struggles, Worries, Happiness, Sadness:

1. Challenges – Taking a chance.
2. Struggles – Non-pleasures that are temporary.
3. Worries – A misuse of imagination.
4. Happiness – Riding life and life is working for you.
5. Sadness – We are always trying to run away from our sadness.

Happy and Sad

Happy and Sad is a cycle; they both are in service for you.

1. Happy is a feeling to let you know that things in life are going great.
2. Sad is a feeling to let you know that things in life are going wrong.

Happy and Sad are only feelings to let you know how you are feeling toward someone or something.

Society Vs. Religion

Society:

1. Tells us what to wear.
2. Tells us what to values to have.
3. Tells us how to act.
4. Tells us what to do.

Religion:

5. Tells us what to wear.
6. Tells us what to values to have.
7. Tells us how to act.
8. Tells us what to do.

Society and Religion are kinds of similar, but:

1. Society - tells us that our reward is MONEY.
2. Religion – tells us that our reward is life after death with GOD.

It all boils down to either GOD or MONEY.

Society System:

In society, people are going to school to learn how to work and how to get money, and they reward at the end is money, house, car, etc. This system is what keeps society going.

This system is what creates "Hope."

Religion System:

In Religion, people are going to church to learn to give to others and to treat others right, to be with GOD, and be rewarded everlasting life, after this life.

This system is what creates "Hope" also.

Hope – is an "Energy" created by us.

Society and Religion both let the people decide with one offer the best for their lives.

Society:

Society is also a religion, but we don't see it.

1. What we want to be comes from society.
2. Society dictates who we should be.
3. Society tells us what to believe in and what we should think of.

The truth is that Society already has our lives mapped out.

Let's say that your life span is 80 years (Break down)

1. You will sleep for about 20 years of your life.
2. You will go to school for nearly ten years to 14 years of your life.
3. You will use the bathroom, getting rid of unused food and bathing and hygiene for about seven years to ten years.
4. You will eat, have fun and be happy for about 20 years
5. You will work for about 20 years.

It's not for everyone, it's just something to think about.

Religion:

Religion doesn't care about your social life.

Religion just wants us to be kind to each other, and to give to each other, then wait for everlasting life after death.

All Society wants us to do is get MONEY, but Religion is about the afterlife.

We all worry so much about life, but unfortunately, we will never beat life. We will have to die.

Society and Religion are just only a "Product" that was created by us.

So, the two most important days in our lives are the day we were born, and the day we will die.

The bottom line is that we are living in a Money System, and we are living to obtain money to survive.

Money moves life. Money is what gets us up in the morning. Having money is what gives us confidence.

We live in a Society System that is already decided for us. If we go out of this system, society will call us "crazy." But society does allow us outside the system by granting us the right of Religion because religion helps society control the people.

Release – Answer

www.releaseanswer.com

Lesson #23 Memory

There are more than five senses:

1. Seeing – What it looks like?
2. Hearing – What it sounds like?
3. Tasting – What it tastes like?
4. Touching – What it feels like?
5. Smelling – What it smells like?
6. Pain – What pain do it have?
7. Time – What time is it?
8. Temperature – What temperature is it?
9. Balance – Do it balance or equal?
10. Fear – Should I beware?

All memories are made from these senses.

Memory – is the evidence of what we gather from the outside of ourselves, to give to our brain, to store it for future use, just like a computer.

Our mind is only a stage for our thoughts. Some of our thoughts make it, and other thoughts will never make it. (Just like sperm cells that never make it to the egg and die). The thoughts that do make it becomes a memory.

Memory was made to capture our thoughts, feelings, actions, and behavior towards what we must deal with within this world and society.

Memory is like a camera. For the brain to take a picture (make a memory) it must examine to see if it is worth keeping. If it is worth keeping, it becomes a memory. If it is not worth keeping it, it gets dissolved.

A memory needs four elements:

1. Learning
2. Decoding
3. Consolidation
4. Retrieval

Memory Explained:

First, information is needed through seeing, hearing and feeling, which is "Learning." Once the information is presented, the brain then needs to represent it to figure out the pattern of seeing, hearing and feeling. When the brain makes sense of it, the pattern starts "decoding" and turns into a picture. Once it is decoded, it gets "consolidated" for long-term use. It then becomes available for "retrieval" at any time in the future

Memory is learning your information.

Release – Answer

www.releaseanswer.com

Lesson #24 Fear

Fear is a tool used to control people.

Fear pulls you back from life.

Fear is a weakness.

Fear makes you lose power.

Fear means, you have no confidence.

Fear is the mind-killer.

Fear is the product of your imagination. Believe it or not, everything you want is on the other side of fear. The greatest fear in the world is from the opinions of others.

Fear contains information about what you fear, and it always encourages you to give up.

Fear is not an object that flows through our system; it is just a "thought." Fear is a beware thought.

There are fears of:

1. Loss
2. Death
3. God
4. Being Alone
5. Being Beaten

Fear is the thief of dreams.

Fear is the oldest and strongest emotion of humankind.

Fear is about possibilities; it is not about the things that happen; it's about the things that might occur.

How to overcome fear:

1. Separate your fears and work on them.
2. Never say that you can't do something.
3. Whatever it is you're scared of doing, just do it.
4. Don't run from difficulty.

There will always be people willing to hurt you, put you down, talk about you, and judge your soul, but don't let it fear you. Tell people around you to keep their fears to themselves.

Having no fear = "Freedom."

Release – Answer

www.releaseanswer.com

Lesson #25 Life Brings Forth Changes

When you start loving yourself and respecting the time and energy you put into your life, "things will change."

When you discover your true worth, your value will go up.

To get better results in life, you must change what you believe about yourself. You must be willing to create something new in your life.

Every day presents a new opportunity to grow.

As you change, you will become:

1. What you think about
2. What you focus on
3. What you read about
4. What you talk about

If you are not happy with yourself, it's time for a new path.

You will never know the best you because you did not create yourself, but if you do things to make yourself happy, you will be creating the best you, which is the beginning of "Change."

You are who you are because of the decisions in life you're made. All your energy that runs through your body each day is needed to get things done. But at the end of the day, your energy dies out to allow you to recharge. That energy rides your life each day. That recharge is freedom.

You need that freedom from energy to relax. The biggest change in life is when you go to sleep. The second biggest change in life is shifting from trying to figure something out, to "actually figuring it out."

Everything in life is always in the process of either coming into being or expiring. So, things in life never remain the same; it keeps moving and changing because there is new energy born every second. Even seconds keep turning into minutes, minutes turn into hours, hours turn into days. Kids to adults. Happy to sad. Open to close and up to down.

Keep challenging yourself, and keep in mind that you do not need anyone's approval to change yourself.

Release – Answer

www.releaseanswer.com

Lesson #26 Hard Work Vs. Luck

Hard work means putting a lot of effort into our projects. Luck means things happening by chance rather than through our efforts.

Often, luck means something good that has happened to us seemingly by pure fortune rather than anything we did.

Luck and hard work can seem like opposites, but they often are linked more closely than you might think. Luck is a positive force that causes good things to happen in our lives. We do hard work to get the desired results.

Hard work vs. luck.

How are hard work and luck related? Below are a few ways in which hard work and luck can be compared with each other.

- We get opportunities because of luck. We work hard to convert those opportunities into realities.

- Hard work can give us more of a sense of personal satisfaction. On the other hand, luck feels more like an unexpected gift.

- Hard work can bring its own 'luck' in the form of unexpected benefits. Under such circumstances, hard work can make us feel lucky.

- Sometimes, luck can advance us much further than hard work alone could. However, if we do not work hard, we might not be able to take full advantage of our luck.

- It is said that "luck favors them who work hard." We should never think that we do not need to work hard. Remember, working hard is pre-requisites for success.

- We can feel lucky that we can work hard, too (for instance, we are lucky that we are not too ill to work).

- Luck can make us feel that there is a divine power rewarding us. Such feelings or thoughts should be taken as positive suggestions to work hard.

Release – Answer

www.releaseanswer.com

Lesson #27 The Science of Mathematics

Math is used to build things and to figure out things. Without math, it is impossible to comprehend this life. Because math makes life seems simple.

Math frees the unknown answers of the universe.

Math is a system to solve life's problems and to calculate all the products in life.

History:

At the beginning of life, we were searching for patterns to understand our lives better.

In the beginning, we watched the days turn into nights, and nights turn back into day; we watched the seasons change and weather change.

After observing these patterns, we discovered "Time."

For us to call this pattern "Time," we had to find a way to calculate the "Time."

At first, we used our fingers and toes; each finger and toe were given a name. We also invented hourglasses with sand in it to measure each hour. Then we developed the evidence that we all have:

1. Two legs
2. Two ears
3. Two feet
4. Two fingers the same
5. Two holes in our nose

Then everything we did was by Twos. Then we all pulled together to create numbers.

Numbers started from:

1. Checkmarks
2. Bones
3. Drawings
4. Rocks
5. Other Materials

History of Numbers:

1. Roman numerals were the first discovery.
2. Brahmi numerals were the second discovery.
3. Hindu Arabic numerals gave us numbers 1-9, and we still use them today.
4. India gave us (0) to be a place holder to record higher numbers.

These are also the numbers we use currently.

Moving on, to evolve as humans, we needed to figure out a system. So, we invented "Math."

We invented math to measure things; by measuring things, we created the meaning for it.

Math created:

1. Time
2. Calculating
3. Counting
4. Measurements
5. Memory
6. Arithmetic Operations

Math's primary function is to find the balance and truth of all things. In other words, math represents the "Truth." Math makes the answer – "Proof," and the product of facts.

Math:

1. (+) = Combines
2. (x) = Repeats
3. (-) = Deducts
4. (divide) = Separates
5. (%) = Percentage

Arithmetic:

Arithmetic = (+), (-), (x), (divide), (%).

Arithmetic = "Build & Destroy"

Algebra:

Algebra = (+), (-), (x), (divide), (%), predicting amounts, predicting balances.

Algebra = "Structure of Operations"

Geometry:

Geometry = Measurements of shapes and figures helps to build and construct.

Geometry = "Properties of Space"

Trigonometry:

Trigonometry = Helps make computers, technology, space travel.

Trigonometry = "Surveying Navigation"

Calculus:

Calculus = Predicts the future, predicts stocks, calculates space travel, defines motion and change.

Calculus = "Rate of Change"

Statistics:

Statistics = Gives us probability, predictions, educated guesses.

Statistics = "Numerical Facts Analysis"

Probability:

Probability = Taking chances, overcoming fear, making a chance to receive something.

Probability = "Risk-Taking"

(Thought), Calculus is the most important of all because it brought us "Motion & Change."

Through "Motion & Change," we discovered that electric (+) magnet = Electro Magnetic Waves.

Which helped us discover:

1. Radios
2. Televisions
3. Cell Phones
4. Computers
5. Stoves
6. Refrigerators
7. Washing Machines
8. Heaters
9. Dryers
10. Lamps
11. Microwaves
12. GPS

Math helps us understand things that enable us to have a memory of it.

Math is how memory was invented. Memory is very calculated.

Math is now a product of everybody's "MIND." With math, we can solve our problems.

Through math, each problem that is solved becomes a rule which serves to solve other problems, which = "Memory."

Math makes things simpler to suit our purposes and to meet our needs.

Math helps us communicate ideas with each other.

What we need math for:

1. To work computers
2. To use the internet
3. To use our cell phones
4. Play music
5. Drive a car
6. Read a clock
7. Fly a plane
8. To count
9. To go to school
10. To invent something new

Math is just an idea, and unfortunately, math is not universal because it doesn't have the formula of "Life & Death", and it cannot calculate everything ever. However, math is the best thing used to measure Life's creations.

Math helps us to discover the way our minds work.

Math is used as a tool to make predictions about the real world we live in.

Math makes us feel that it is something there before we even get what we are looking for.

So, actually, "Math" = "Memory"

Every time we learn something, we must break it down mathematically to store it in our brain.

Lesson #28 Understanding Math

Math's job is to find patterns to represent how things happen and how things work.

Math is about seeing what happens when you put two or more things together.

All the Laws of nature are now written in the language of "Math."

Let's start on our journey, first, we must know that:

1. Now = Light, sound, energy, thought + instant.
2. Day = Sun-up, minus sun-down + space.

We have seven days from religious theories. There are no breaks in sunrise and sunset; humans just decided to stop at seven days to create time.

No matter what, there will always be a sunrise and sunset until there are no people alive to see it.

Man created time, days, months, and years to keep track of his history.

Math is learned patterns, and its job is to find more patterns to govern what we see.

Math is a language that allows people to communicate with each other through patterns.

Math allows us to do our everyday things through patterns.

Math has given us all the opportunity to play the game of "Life" better.

Math is solving a complex problem to make life easier.

Math is also a part of "Success."

Success:

1. **Math**
2. **Life**
3. **Opportunity**

Math is always present in everyone's "Success."

Release – Answer

Lesson #29 Thinking with Math

Math keeps all our thoughts organized.

Math is the front line of learning and reasoning.

Math helps us organize the choices that are available to us.

Math helps us store all the information in our brains.

Math calculates all our "habits".

We are all made by our habits.

Here are some of our habits:

1. Walking
2. Talking
3. Moving
4. Drinking
5. Smoking
6. Combing our hair
7. Taking showers
8. Using the restroom
9. Using the internet
10. Using our cell phone

Thinking is our biggest Habit of all. Habits put us into a cycle that governs our lives. Within that habit cycle, we developed reasoning.

Reasoning is observing patterns, then concluding.

Reasoning:

  a) Here is the information.
  b) What did you get out of it?
  c) The conclusion is based on what you think it is.

All your conclusions become routine thoughts, and all those routine thoughts will train and guide all your future thoughts.

So, learning is only training ourselves, and we earn what we learn.

Release – Answer

Lesson #30 Reticular Activating System

Math has designed our "Reticular Activating System."

Our Reticular Activating System is a filter system that allows only certain information to enter our brain. It also blocks out unwanted information.

Guess who programmed that filter? "YOU and MATH"

How it was made:

1. From all the things you have been going through in your life.
2. From the people in your past information.
3. From all the information you have heard and seen in your life.

The Reticular Activating System job is to look for evidence to confirm if you need the information or not. The system is made not to let everything enter your brain.

If the brain took in every information at equal value, your head would explode.

The Reticular Activating System protects our brain by filtering information and only letting in the information that it agrees with.

The Reticular Activating System (RAS) is in the base of our brain.

The RAS acts as a filter against all data that is around us, like:

1. Sounds
2. Tastes
3. Colors
4. Images
5. Pictures

These things can add up to 2,000.000 bits of data at any given time.

Our RAS filter only lets information into our brain that it thinks is important.

How does the RAS know what is essential?

Answer: It measures what we focus on the most.

Example:

Let's say that you always focus on saying, "I can't lose weight." The RAS will take that thought and look for information so that you will never lose weight again.

Let's say that you say, "I'm always late." The RAS will get information to make sure that you will always be late.

Be very careful what you focus on because you will attract what you focus on.

Bad focuses:

1. I am terrible at this.
2. There are not enough hours in the day.
3. I always mess things up.
4. I never have enough money.

If you keep focusing on these kinds of thoughts, your RAS will show you information to prove that those are true for you.

Set your RAS to look for positive focuses as:

1. I am great at this.
2. I am always on time.
3. I am confident.
4. I am good with money.

Just focus on what you are good at, then your RAS will start to show you information to prove that your beliefs are right for you.

Remember this:

What you think about, you bring about.

Your mind is just like a garden, whatever you plant will grow.

Over a million things are going on around you, but you are not tuned in to all of it.

Your RAS decides what is going to come into your mind.

Deep Learning

Thoughts:

1. We use information to give rise to new thoughts.
2. We use information to change the way we think each day.

Intelligence:

1. Intelligence is nothing special; it only means that you follow the rules of something that is information, as fast and efficiently as possible.
2. Intelligence is not enough, you need to be a rule-breaker and a game-changer, crazy and creative too.

The brain calculates 500 times a second. The computer calculates 3.4 billion times a second. The reason why the computer calculates so high is that there are billions of brains (people) operating it each day.

Learning is nothing special, learning is great, but deep understanding is better.

When we learn something, we can unlearn it, but once we understand it, we cannot de-understand it again. Because understanding means that you change the way you process information.

Stress:

Stress comes from the things we cannot do anything about it.

Stress is thinking about information we don't know about.

Now, how do we program our RAS:

1. Create a want
2. Keep reminding yourself about the want
3. Then act

Remember, whatever you plant is what you will get.

Now, how do we program everyone's RAS:

1. You must market and advertise what you want everyone to do.
2. You must get everyone's attention on you.
3. You must tell them what you need from them.

So, focus on what you want and need in life, and you will attract it to you.

Release – Answer

www.releaseanswer.com

Lesson #31 Logic

Thoughts are in everything we do. There will always be thoughts if people have ideas.

Thoughts are "ideas."

Thoughts are well structured, but it must go through a process called reasoning.

Reasoning – judges the thoughts.

Reasoning:

1. It questions the thought.
2. It asks us why we need the thought in the first place.
3. It measures the truth of the thought.

To "lie" or tell the "truth," you must have a reason to.

All actions have a reason behind it.

We must have a reason to do everything we do.

True or False

True = Proof + Belief.

The more proof we see about something, the stronger we believe it to be true.

Things can only be true or false, never both at the same time.

True and false can never be in the same space at the same time.

Logic:

Logic is the science or study of thinking and reasoning. It's what is outside of everyday reality. It's what is outside of life's "Living Box." You must think outside of yourself.

Logic thinking for 2020:

1. What're the reasons for this thought?
2. Is this thought true or false.
3. Is there a better thought?

Math calculates what we think and Logic reasons what we think.

"Thinking" is a challenging conception of our imagination to be judged by ourselves.

Release – Answer

www.releaseanswer.com

Lesson #32 The Business of Thinking

Thinking – is a process of structuring information and doing something with it.

Thinking is ideas, and the ideas we hold are not ours, it comes from the information we find.

We are all made of data, and we have a full collection of information stored in our brain from outside data input.

The data is composed of:

1. Instructions
2. Rules
3. Challenges
4. Changes
5. Questions
6. Hopes
7. Promises

The data that we decide to let enter our brain becomes memories, and our previous and present experiences help us to structure our memories.

Challenges:

When we challenge anything around us, we are trying to punish all mistakes.

Challenge = how many ways can we see the situation for what it is.

Education:

Education = when we do something new that we didn't do before and we have learned a lesson from it.

We have spent years and years in schools and Universities to learn what other people have thought, discovered and created, which proves that we are all programmed, how to think and what to think.

Every time we try to think outside of education, and can't find an answer to something, we kill our ideas and then run back to education, where it is safe.

Education = inside the box.

Inside the box, we agree with others because it is safe in it. But whatever is outside of the box is invisible to us because we don't know what is outside. We believe that outside the box is very risky.

We must think outside the box to do things our way, not the way everyone else does.

We believe that outside the box is fear, but fear is manufactured by ourselves, and it is a lie.

We also believe that outside the box is worry, but worry is only thinking of all the things we fear and don't want to happen to us.

If your life sucked five years ago and it still sucks today, it is primary evidence that you cannot figure out how to get out of the box. **Take a risk and get out of the box.**

Our success and failures are what make us who we are.

How we act and feel comes from the things we encounter that are hard for us to deal with and understand. What we already know helps us to understand what we haven't still thought about yet.

If there is a problem, we need to solve it by finding the success and failure of it.

The difference between success and failure is:

1. Success is solving problems.
2. Failure is just problems.

Success becomes a success after it solves the problem.

To solve a problem, we must do something way different, then what we were doing, if what we were doing didn't work.

Conclusion:

1. In the box = we must follow the only choices available to us.
2. Outside the box = We create our own choices.

Create your own choices in the business of thinking.

Lesson #33 Something to Think About

Something to think about:

1. If you give something, you will have less.
2. When you are thinking about something, your mind is also thinking about something else.
3. Every answer will create more questions.
4. The mind is always seeing and searching for some meaning in life
5. Doubt helps our intelligence; it sharpens it.
6. Death kills the past, which mean everyday dies.
7. All workers are brought for whatever their salaries are.
8. All answers to "why" are information.
9. Opinions are usually something which people have when they don't have an answer.
10. Books deliver information.
11. Trade isn't about money and goods; trade is about information.
12. Money only sits in the bank or wallet, until information moves it.
13. Goods sit in the warehouse until information moves it.
14. No matter how much information we use to describe something, it will always be incomplete.
15. The only complete description of something is the thing itself.
16. Facebook = asks what's on your mind.
17. Twitter = asks you what's going on.

18. LinkedIn = wants you to re-connect with colleagues.
19. YouTube = tells you what to watch.
20. When we cry, we are crying out bad information.
21. Information is controlled because we were not born with information.
22. Our problem is that we worry about what we know and don't know too much.
23. People only want to be with you, because of how you make them feel and for what you can do for them.
24. If you fuck up, you must make up.
25. When people say, "everything happens for a reason," they are saying, "I can't understand why this is happening."
26. When people say, "A thing must have a good in it," they are really saying, "Right now it is not good,"
27. What is, is, and what isn't we make it what it is.
28. We don't lose, we either win or learn.
29. Whatever data or substance we put into ourselves, we will feel something about it.
30. What you know isn't shit, you must have proof.
31. Everything around us is energy, and we have the power to control it with our thoughts.
32. A man will never be appropriately treated if he has no money.
33. We let people borrow us to better their lives.

Lesson #34 Here & Now

All our lives, we have never been accepted for who we are. Everyone has been trying to put improvements upon us to try to make us better.

As a result, it has made us feel:

1. "I'm not good enough as I am."
2. "Something must be missing."

People are always telling us; we are not good enough. This feeling has become our first sign of fear. Our fear of not being good enough started our worries. When we become aware of fear, we become aware of more concerns.

Fear = problems

There are always problems around us, but we just don't see them.

The problems that we can see, we have learned to postpone them because we are afraid of solving them right away.

What we need to know at this day and time is that out of each problem, we are going to gain something from it.

Problems kill our time, and it creates worry. Our biggest worry is thinking about the future; it wastes our present time.

All we have is the present moment, which is "Here & Now." If we think about yesterday or tomorrow, we will only worry.

Yesterday & Tomorrow:

1. Yesterday – is no more, it died.
2. Tomorrow – is not here yet, it hasn't lived yet.

When we only think about this moment, all worries disappear.

We are only given one moment at a time, and we waste that moment in planning or worrying about the future or past. Each moment is born out of this moment.

We are never in the "Now" because we are always worrying about later or the past. Which makes us absent from "Now." Each "Now" = a second.

Life is available for us right "Now," but we are always too busy and unavailable for it.

Remember this:

"Death will kill all of our "Now's" if we don't use our "Now's" wisely.

Sun-up to Sun-down and Sun-down to Sun-up again = 1,440 "Now's".

So, each day we are losing 1,440 "Now's" of our lives, worrying about the future and past.

The Process of Worrying:

Worrying brings us to the word "Fuck." 'Fuck" is the most significant worrying word of all time.

"Fuck" has become the most important word in our language; it can define:

1. Pain
2. Pleasure
3. Hate
4. Love

Uses:

1. Ignorance = Fuck if I know
2. Trouble = I guess I'm fucked now
3. Fraud = I got fucked
4. Aggression = Fuck you!
5. Displeasure = What the fuck is going on here
6. Difficulty = I can't understand this fucking shit
7. Incompetence = He is a fuck off
8. Suspicion = What the fuck are you doing
9. Enjoyment = I had a fucking good time
10. Request = Get the fuck out of here
11. Hostility = I'm going to knock your fucking head off
12. Greeting = How the fuck are you
13. Apathy = Who gives a fuck
14. Innovation = Get a bigger fucking hammer
15. Surprise = fuck, you scared the fuck out of me
16. Anxiety = Today is really fucked up
17. Lust = Can I fuck you

We must focus on "Here & Now." Don't use your time as a waiting period; use your time wisely because death will never give it back.

Lesson #35 Believing Vs. Knowing

Believing and knowing are two different things.

Believing:

1. We are still searching for more data.
2. We believe until we can know for our self.
3. We have not figured something out yet.
4. It's not 100% yet.
5. We still have some doubt about it.
6. We don't have all the evidence yet.

Believing is knowing something that we cannot understand through math, science, and history.

Believing is the faith in knowing the things we believe in.

Belief is just a thought of trust, faith, and hope until we know it to be the truth.

Belief is just being convinced until we are sure.

Sometimes, belief can be wrong. So, it would be wise to stop believing and start "Knowing."

Knowing:

1. Is the right answer.
2. It's not an estimate.
3. Knowing it is having it.
4. It's proof.
5. It's 100% correct.
6. It's having no doubt.
7. It's having evidence to back it up.

We should work on what we know, not on what we think we know. Because what we think we know can change, but what we know, will never change unless we didn't know it.

We only know what we were told to be true and what was taught to us to be true.

The truth is that we must find the truth of things, and we must find the truth to knowing before we get caught up with just beliefs.

If we know something, it means "It is," which means it's true.

"Knowing is truth, and "Not knowing" is 0% of what you may think it is until you know it for yourself.

What you know comes from whatever you give your heart too.

Release – Answer

www.releaseanswer.com

Lesson #36 Common Sense

Common Sense = Basic Logic.

Every day there are all kinds of rules we must follow:

1. Take showers
2. Brush our teeth
3. Urinate and get rid of waste
4. Eat and drink
5. While driving, stop at the red light, and go when the light turns green
6. Use a pen to write with
7. Use a spoon, fork, and knife to eat with
8. Put on clothes
9. Call and receive calls on our cell phone
10. Keep up with time
11. Remember what we must do
12. Being careful while we are walking and driving

These are the things we do that allow us to calculate and reason.

Calculating = Determining

Reasoning = Arguing

Every time we obey a rule, we get information from it. That information is distributed to our brains. Then the brain permits us to understand it. The brain then gives us a memory to hold the understanding.

If there is something that we can't wrap our brain around, we look to our common sense.

Common Sense:

Common Sense = The total of our life experiences.

Common Sense = Realizing + Belief

Common Sense holds:

1. Good judgments
2. Bad judgments
3. Happiness
4. Sickness
5. Sadness
6. Angriness
7. Truths
8. Lies
9. Progress
10. Defeats
11. Battles

When we call on our Common Sense, it means we don't know what's right about what we are thinking about.

Common Sense is seeing things as they are and using past experiences as a reference to help.

How do we find out what's good or bad?

Answer: We must experience the feeling or thought or find belief or evidence about it.

A lot of people would say that we have to feel what is good or bad, but that is not true because if we feel like hitting someone who has hurt our feelings, the feeling of hitting them will make us feel good. That's because we have fought for our feelings. Is that good or bad? If we just think of hitting the person and not do it. Is that good or bad?

The feeling of PEACE:

Poor people are always trying to grow up to live right to find peace:

1. Sex = Peace
2. Truth = Peace
3. Freedom = Peace

75% of Human believes there is a GOD which will give them peace after death.

We are all searching for our peace.

We, as humans, were born in a belief system, and we never asked anyone for proof. With a lack of evidence, all our beliefs have become our reality.

Common Sense is a circle within us:

In this circle, we have everything we have learned and all the knowledge we have acquired.

This circle represents all the knowledge we have gathered throughout our lives.

Every time we learn something, we put it in our circle.

If we try to put in our circle what we already know, we wouldn't learn anything.

We must put new information into our circle to learn.

The next level:

We have all been programmed to immediately reject what we hear and see that is not inside our circle.

The wiser people on our planet have learned that we will not progress until we commit ourselves to the next level, which is learning outside of the circle.

For us to get to the next level, we must conquer our feelings of "being pleased" and "being worried."

The next level = getting information outside of our circle to feed our Common Sense.

We must stay away from negative people that pull us down because negative people only contaminate our energy. We must get rid of negative people to purify our Common Sense.

Things to put into our circle (Common Sense):

1. Don't let other people waste your time.
2. Keep real things away from false things.
3. Listen by the moment and see by the second.
4. Religion is just like a drug.
5. Truth = a belief ruled by what we have decided it to be.

Today young Common Sense is more advance then old Common Sense, because of computers.

Conclusion:

Our lives are just borrowed here on Earth. We have all became prisoners of life until our lives are over. People come into life, then build up their Common Sense, then die off.

Release – Answer

www.releaseanswer.com

Lesson #37 Temporary

Temporary = Comes & Goes.

All the things we see are subject to change.

Nothing is made to last forever.

Whatever people have invented, we just rent the idea for as long as we can.

Temporary things:

1. Our bodies
2. Our jobs
3. People
4. Time
5. Laws
6. Friends
7. Pets
8. Being a baby
9. Sickness
10. Problems
11. Angriness
12. Depression
13. Sadness
14. Happiness
15. Madness
16. Fearful
17. Accidents
18. Crying
19. Thinking
20. Feelings
21. Worrying
22. Life

Between life and death = space.

Within this space is:

1. Animals
2. Vegetables
3. Minerals
4. Metal
5. Materials
6. Oxygen
7. Water
8. Sun
9. Moon
10. Fire

These are the elements of life and they are all temporary.

Don't focus on temporary things because you will not find inner peace.

You will not have inner peace if you attach short-term things to your life.

Temporary things don't create long-term peace.

Inner peace = Long-term peace.

If we temporarily put things and people in our lives for short-term, we shouldn't expect long-term peace.

Don't get me wrong; we will feel good when we put things and people in our short-term space, but when things and people are taken away from us, we will feel unhappy. There will be a repeated process of trying to replace that feeling with something or someone else all that time.

We must try to find a long-term situation to satisfy our life between life and death.

Here are some temporary things that can become long-term:

Positive:

1. Smiling
2. Love
3. Growing
4. Learning
5. Starting something

Negative:

1. Drinking
2. Smoking
3. Drugging
4. Stinking
5. Stealing
6. Lying
7. Hitting

Neutral:

1. Open can be closed at anytime
2. Up can come down at anytime
3. In can come out at anytime
4. Far can come near at anytime
5. Good can become bad at anytime
6. Love can become hate at any giving time

How to find long-term situations?

1. Disconnect the things you don't care about.
2. Re-evaluate all your relationships and focus on who is there for you for the long-term.
3. Things and people who get in the way of your success eliminate them or it.

Connection:

1. Connect to things and people that can build up your success.
2. Disconnect all liabilities immediately.
3. A connection is understanding what you want.

Temporary things:

1. Not lasting or permanent.
2. Not needed for very long.
3. Lasting for only a limited time.
4. Serving or enjoyed for a limited time.

Within our short-term time here on Earth, we should only try to enjoy ourselves.

Lesson #38 What Fits into Life

There are four fits in life:

1. Fit = Natural grade A people you get along with, they are suitable proper and becoming.
2. Unfit = Unqualified people that are not physically fit and unsuitable.
3. Misfit = People that are unable to adjust to the circumstances of their situation.
4. Counterfeit = People who are not real, not genuine, fake and imitations.

We all come from one of these fits.

The bottom line is that we, as people, are not perfect, and we will never be perfect. Because perfect is just an illusion, it will never show up to play.

Life is about image:

1. Our mother and father gave us a name.
2. Society mode us.
3. People gave us ideas.
4. Religion gave us hope.
5. The Government gave us rules.
6. Then we had to develop our own identity to survive.

Who are we?

We are trying to be something for this World, we call life.

We are all just actors of our own lives.

What keeps us alive is; we don't think we are the person we need to be.

The truth is that whatever we put our attention to will become our life. Because everything we do in our lives, we have the energy for it.

Our lives are just a printout of our actual behaviors.

We all live in three different worlds at the same time:

1. World of thoughts
2. World of feelings
3. World of emotions

All three worlds have hurt attached to it.

"Hurt gives us information."

Hurt = when you hear something, with your ears, and expect to see the same with your eyes and you don't.

Hurt brings us to worry.

Worry = praying for something that we don't want.

Thoughts, feelings, and emotions combined are what give us the ability to create life.

As we create life, we bring forth other people into existence.

The newly created life we bring into existence will have no choice but to contribute to what we have accomplished so far.

Cells:

Our cells within us are over Fifty trillion cells.

If you think about it, we are not just a single entity (person); we are an individual community of 50 trillion cells.

Every cell is like a battery.

Every cell is intelligent, but when the cells are in a community, they give up their intelligence and respond to the central voice, "your mind."

So, we must program our minds to set up the environment for our cell community.

How do we program our minds?

Stop saying:

1. I can't do it.
2. I don't have the time.
3. I'm tired.

These are just ways to escape.

What we need to program in our minds are:

1. How can I do it?
2. How can I make time for it?
3. How can I get motivated?

Facts:

Negative = Statements (which closes the mind).

Positive = Questions (Which opens the mind).

If we are willing to find the answer to a question, we will always "think."

"Thinking will always keep our mind programmed."

Control:

Everybody wants us to come into their box (their life & mind), so they can control us.

But our job is to not go into their box (their life & mind), we must make them come into our box (our life & mind).

How do we know when someone is trying to put us into their box?

Answer:

We will have bad vibes immediately.

Thoughts:

1. When we are having thoughts, we are activating things in the world that are connected to our thoughts.
2. Languages were designed to hide feelings.
3. When we do something wrong, who rules are we breaking.
4. Pills don't heal us; it's the thought of taking them that heals us.
5. Money = Energy.
6. Giving away our money is giving away a piece of our life.
7. Human created marriage.
8. We belong to ourselves, but we do let other people borrow us from time to time.

We all are forced to live the way we live.

Lesson #39 Paying Attention

Education = Information.

Information = Something that was not yours, that you have attached to you, to form a memory.

Attention:

1. Attention appears to be the mechanism when our brain focuses.
2. Attention = the experience of observing.
3. Attention is directing the mind to an object.

When we direct our attention to something, we are directing our brain to focus on it.

Wondering:

1. Wondering kills attention.
2. Our minds are wondering about 47% of the time.
3. Wondering is where we do all our creative thinking and planning.
4. When our mind is wondering, we seem to be less happy, then when we are focused.

To be able to pay attention, we must cut off wondering about other things that do not matter and direct our attention to something; we must pay attention too.

How do we pay attention?

Answer:

1. By not wasting our time and energy with losers.
2. By paying 100% attention to things that will benefit us.

Example:

If you get 70% on a test, it would mean that you have only contributed 70% attention to it.

If you get 100% on a test, it would mean that you have contributed 100% attention to it.

Paying Attention:

People contribute more attention to things like:

1. Mary had a little lamb
2. The cow jumped over the moon
3. Santa Clause
4. Easter Bunny
5. Tooth Ferry
6. Cartoons
7. Things that are make-believe

These days, people only contribute attention to emergencies.

What we should be contributing our attention to:

1. Observing how people treat us, so we will be able to understand, who is for us and who is against us.
2. Observe what we are eating, so we don't get sick.
3. Observe what people are really saying to us.

You ever wondered why some people have more opportunities than others.

Answer:

They can see things that other people cannot see because they "Pay Attention" to details.

Everything has a set of strategies that we can tap into if we only "Pay Attention" to it.

Remember this:

1. Failure is what we don't know.
2. Knowledge is only a conclusion about our imaginations.
3. Happiness, Sadness, Hurt and Fear, happen only in the here and now, and if we don't "Pay Attention," it will keep happening to us beyond the here and now.

So, "Paying Attention" is the greatest power of Life.

Lesson #40 Life is a Business

We use past experiences of life as a basis for deciding whether something is possible or not possible or whether something is right or wrong.

Everyone has a life of their own.

Sun-up until sun-down and sun-down until sun-up is only a space that has light and darkness.

That space is not 'Time.' The truth is we are "Time."

We are born with our own built-in "Time."

Our energy has a certain time to live unless something can kill our energy sooner than expected.

Everyone has their own time in their reality.

It takes people time to get to our present time, because they would have to leave their own current time, to enter ours. We enter and exit other people's lives every day. People enter and exit our lives every day, also.

Our energy within us moves about 100 miles per second or 1000 miles per hour within us.

We have slowed "Life" down to 3,600 seconds per hour to see what we are doing.

Proof:

1. If we are in a car moving 60 miles per hour, can we still think?
2. If we are on a plane moving 450 to 650 miles per hour, can we still think?

Life can increase and decrease in speed.

Our lives are traveling the distance to our death.

Living is energy, and our energy is our "Life."

Time doesn't tick away; our lives are what ticks away.

We are all just an individual life with:

1. Thoughts from what we have learned.
2. Opinions from what we have learned.
3. Feelings from things we encountered.
4. Memories from our understandings.

We all exist for Four reasons:

1. We live to contribute to our memories.
2. We live to learn from our mistakes.
3. We live for our imaginations.
4. We live to see what other people will imagine for the next day.

Memories make us worry, and worries keep us alive. If we all stop worrying, there wouldn't be anything to do.

Everyone wants to live forever, but there is not enough time within us to live forever.

Forever only belongs to our imaginations.

Here are some facts:

1. 100% of people born 200 years ago are all dead.
2. Information is for those who don't know it yet.
3. Everything is a problem until you know it.
4. Once you believe in something, your eyes become wide open to it.
5. The way you think is the way you feel.
6. Things you hear, see and feel are the only things that can hurt you.
7. Being calm in tough situations is a "Superpower."
8. Being deceive by someone is not hurting until you continue to remember it.
9. All things have formulas to make it what it is.
10. We decide what we will care for.
11. Arguing will destroy all the relaxation you have.
12. Your mind keeps changing its direction, because of different thoughts and feelings.
13. Arguments are for approval and disapproval.

What we want to do in life is what we like, then we must go through a process to get it.

We would have to earn it.

Everything earns a living:

1. Human
2. Animals
3. Birds
4. Insects
5. Fish
6. Flowers
7. Trees

Happy Vs. Unhappy:

We feel unhappy because life is not happening the way we want it to happen.

So, if life is not happening the way we think it should happen, we become unhappy.

On the other hand, if life is happening the way we think it should happen, we become happy.

When we say something is not possible, what we are saying is "I don't want it."

Life is a business because we figured out how to make money from it.

What we invest our lives in is "money."

Money is just a paper that makes us:

1. Fight
2. Lie
3. Steal
4. Kill

Money buys us joy and opportunity.

Some people say, "All we want is money, and we shouldn't be only wanting money."

The truth is, "what else is it to want these days."

1. Love doesn't always last.
2. Material things get boring.
3. Good health doesn't last forever (death is not having any more health again).

What else is here on this planet that is worth something to make you feel happy before you die.

"MONEY"

Lesson #41 Problems About Worrying

We all waste our time worrying.

Worrying is a story that we all create for ourselves.

Every moment of worrying is a waste of our time and energy.

Worrying is the misuse of imagination:

1. Worrying is fear.
2. Worrying is a lack of something.
3. Worrying is worrying about something that has not happened yet.
4. Worrying is a symptom that we think we won't be safe.

Powers of worrying:

1. Wishing is worrying
2. Hoping is worrying
3. Wanting is worrying
4. Thinking is worrying
5. Imagining is worrying
6. Afraid is worrying
7. Nervous is worrying

We all surrender our freedom to worry.

At each moment, we can become anything we wish to be, but when we worry, we choose to be sad.

Bad Worries:

1. Worries can make us sick.
2. Worries drain our resources.
3. Worries are mental false alarms.
4. Worries are false facts.
5. Worries cause panic to our emotional energy.

Worrying is when we imagine that some unwanted thing is going to happen.

Example:

If I ask you; How are you feeling next week?

Your answer will be: "I don't know."

I have made you worried about next week.

Worrying is a waste of our mental space.

Instead of worrying, try to see the problem another way. You are having your problems, only because you can't see the answer yet.

90% of the things you worry about will never happen. The worrying is just your mind running wild.

Stop worrying today, if you need an answer to your worries, go to www.releaseanswer.com to get the answer and solution to your worries, fears, concerns, and problems..

History of Worrying:

First, everyone has three selves:

1. Past Self
2. Present Self
3. Future Self

All selves will be different. They all will have different energies and time frames. They are all addicted to their Energy and Time.

All our three selves are available to us; through our memories, we just have to tap into them.

We all are only visiting this image of living.

Our body is just a costume that we must wear until we must depart this image of living.

Every day we are driving our life through this way of living.

In this image of living, we have made "time, energy, and money the essential living sources.

We must handle all the problems that this image of living is made of.

No matter how big the problems may be, we must continue to live on.

Every day we turn into a different person because each day brings forth changes and choices.

Changes and Choices:

1. Changes make things become, once upon a time.
2. Choices are the most powerful thing we have going for ourselves.

The best thing to do is to focus on what you can control instead of worrying.

Create your environment and learn to control it.

It's not about what you can do, it's more about what you will do.

We only worry about the things we are concern about and care about.

Solutions:

1. A problem just needs to be resolved.
2. We worry because we don't know the truth of it.
3. The greatest gift of all is truth.
4. Truth is just something we can't see at the time, but once we see the truth, we need not seek for it anymore.
5. Once something happens, it is not a worry anymore.
6. Don't just see things for what it is, see it better than it is.
7. Always visualize things going well.
8. Good information, music, and love will keep us from worrying.

Worrying Vs. Confidence:

Confidence:

1. Make something out of each opportunity.
2. Don't fight battles that are not yours.
3. Let go of whatever doesn't serve you.
4. Stop listening to losers; losers can't see your dreams and desires.

(because they are not you)

We have been studying ourselves for thousands of years, and the truth is that we all live in a world that we can only think about. That is the biggest reason why we worry.

We worry about the wrong things:

1. We fall in love with tomorrow, but we hate it when it becomes today.
2. To stop worrying, we must give today more attention than we will give tomorrow.
3. Yesterday's part of your life has died.
4. Faith dies when we get whatever we hoped for.

"Worries are a "dead end."

Life is just a system we have created to keep all of us controlled.

There is a world within us:

1. When we say something, we are defining what we have to say.
2. What we have to say is the definition of what we were thinking and feeling.
3. Whatever we know is the definition of what we have learned.
4. What we don't know is the definition of what we have not learned yet.
5. What we think we know is the definition of what we believe.

We are in an energy base world, and we are just energy that will die one day.

Worrying:

1. Worrying creates doubt.
2. Doubt creates fear.
3. Fear creates bad feelings.
4. Bad feelings create problems.
5. Problems create more problems.

So, we better watch what we think because all our thoughts are addictive to our minds.

Lesson #42 Good Vs. Bad

We all did a lot of good things in life.

We all did a lot of bad things in life.

We all did bad things mainly because we chose to or because we had to.

We wouldn't know what's good if we didn't know bad.

There is an internal program of good and bad running within each one of us.

What's so good about "Bad" is that everyone respects "Bad."

What's so bad about "Good" is that it takes a lot of thinking to be "Good."

Religion uses good and bad for civil control.

The truth is that we are going to do what we must do, whether it is good or bad to survive.

Good and Bad is humanmade. We as people have created good and bad and have planted patterns in our minds.

Example:

If humans never existed, where would good and bad be used.

We must have reasons to be good and bad for good and bad to exist.

We can't be good or bad about something unless we have something to do with it.

Good and Bad are judged by the consequences it generates.

If we look at it carefully, there are no good and bad things. It's the people that perform the actions of good and bad. Some actions produce unfortunate consequences, and some actions produce wonderful outcomes.

Wait a minute; there was a way before both good and bad, which was "Right and Wrong."

Right and Wrong came from past Kings in early history.

Right and Wrong were divided into two sides; then, it became "Good and Bad."

1. Right became: "Good."
2. Wrong became "Bad."

This belief became the Law of Religion.

Good and Bad is only a thought.

Good and Bad are judgments.

Today, intentions to do something can only be Good or Bad.

1. Good is what people prefer in life these days.
2. Bad is what people don't prefer in life these days.

Good and Bad is only a human action.

The truth is that we cannot be good in this kind of World.

Religion:

Religion has brought Good and Bad to the front line of life.

Religion has taught us reasoning and consciences.

Conclusion:

We will do good or bad to get the information we need.

Every thought is humanmade, just as every prescription has a prescriber, and everything made has a creator.

Just focus on who you are, not on who you were. Accept what is and let go of what was.

Lesson #43 Science of Lying

Lying has become a normal thing in life these days.

We are all liars; we are born liars.

Lying is a form of power:

1. We lie when the truth doesn't work.
2. We lie to gain advantage.
3. We lie to paint a better picture of ourselves.
4. We lie to be the person we wish we were.
5. We lie to escape accountability.
6. We lie to avoid punishment.
7. We lie to inflict pain upon people.
8. We lie to steal admiration.
9. We lie to feel better for the moment.
10. We lie because we don't want to admit that we are wrong.
11. We lie to get away with something.
12. We lie because we fear something.
13. We lie to help people.
14. We lie to avoid conflict.
15. We lie to communicate and connect with other people.
16. We lie for pleasure.
17. We lie to hurt other people.
18. We lie to protect other people.
19. We lie to be polite.
20. We lie to not hurt other people feelings.
21. We lie to blame someone else.
22. We lie to protect ourselves.

Lying is a Human tool.

1. We are masters of self-deception.
2. We fool ourselves into believing false things.
3. We refuse to believe the true things.
4. We lie to ourselves over and over because we don't have enough strength to admit the truth and deal with the consequences that will follow.

Lying is part of our lives.

Lying connect our wishes and our fantasies.

Lies:

Lies help us to be who we wish we were and how we wish we could be.

Truth:

1. Truth is honesty.
2. Trust is keeping a promise.
3. True is proven accurate information.

All three Truth, Trust, and True are humanmade.

Our Creator only knows the absolute truth of all things. So, the absolute truth is with our Creator.

There are two truths:

1. The Creators truth.
2. Our truth.

Our reality is only made up of our opinions.

We all get passionate about our truths.

But our truths are only made of our opinions, and our Creator has nothing to do with our opinions. So, we don't even have a clue about the truth of all things.

Process of Lies:

The system to tell a lie, (We need five things):

1. Time
2. Space
3. Truth
4. Doubt
5. A good lie

- Time = sequence
- Space = imagination
- Truth = the truth and nothing but the truth
- Doubt = to be uncertain about something
- A good lie = something believable

Put them all together, and it becomes a system of manufacturing lies.

Communications:

We communicate to:

1. Build relationships.
2. Inform people of things.
3. Entertain people.
4. Persuade people.

When we put the system of lying together with communication, we will get:

1. "Lying is communicating without telling the truth."
2. "Truth is communicating without telling a lie."

Lying is our first thought until we practice enough about telling the truth.

To lie the brain must compare two pieces of information at once:

1. The truth
2. The lie

The mind must eliminate the real part of the information and then tell the lie without displaying any symptoms that we are lying.

Lying:

1. Pretending = putting on an act.
2. Projecting Image = trying to be a different person then you are.
3. Omitting information = falsifying information.

Advantages of lies:

1. A lie promotes our feelings.
2. A lie helps us put ourselves on the top.
3. A lie helps us feel better.
4. A lie makes us feel comfortable.

People lie because being honest is like being on a diet or quitting cigarettes.

Telling the truth is being disciplined.

Even people who are just thinking about lying and decides not to are liars.

We as people cannot stop or control lies, so we decided to just hand over all lies to religion.

Lies will never stop because we will always believe that lies are better than the consequences.

Lies have created a reason to excuse ourselves from what is right.

Liars:

1. Liars sell dreams to people.
2. Liars gain a victory over their victims.
3. Lairs are good listeners.
4. Liars will tell you they are busy to avoid you.
5. Liars offer a quick opportunity to people.

All lies are from the imagination.

All our thoughts and accomplishments are from the imagination.

There is no real truth because our imagination fuels life.

Facts:

If everyone decides to admit the truth on all occasions, the World will change Quickly.

One lie has the power to tarnish a thousand truths. So, how long would it take for the World to be only lies?

Release – Answer

www.releaseanswer.com

Lesson #44 The Science of Everything

The science of everything is "Life," and we don't even know a damn thing about this life.

We don't know when it began nor when it will end.

The truth is, we are just a piece of this Planet until we die.

Which makes life a living platform to experience.

Life:

1. Create Vs. Destroy
2. Grow Vs. Decrease
3. Gain Vs. Lose
4. Live Vs. Die
5. Learn Vs. Ignore
6. Think Vs. Sleep

Life is nothing more than survival.

Survival:

- Suffering
- Hurting
- Sleeping
- Learning
- Eating
- Breathing
- Helping
- Teaching
- Loving
- Hating
- Killing
- Crying
- Laughing
- Sexing
- Ruling
- Listening
- Dying

Overall "life" is:

1. Energy
2. Memory
3. Information
4. Imagination

L = EMII

Life is an experience:

We are born into a life that is already set up by the people that were here before us. They created a system of learning from their understanding of our Planet. Then they taught these learning methods to future generations.

Our thoughts can only think about the things we have learned already.

Everything that exists is only problems that must be solved or discovered.

The reason why there are problems is that there were no instructions that came with our lives.

Today, there are still no signs of instructions, which means that we had to figure out life for ourselves. We, as humans, had to figure out what works best for ourselves.

Every thought comes from our human mind. We are the architects of what we do.

Our accomplishments are about 10,000 years of memory.

We spent these years:

- Studying ourselves.
- Studying the materials on the Planet.
- Studying other animals.
- Learning to survive.
- Setting up a government.
- Starting Religions.

We have survived in a world that we knew nothing about.

I'm about to shack you!

We are in the middle of nothing, and all we know is that we live and die.

Every time a person is born, we fill up the nothing space. Then people die to free up the nothing space for the newborn; if no one dies, there will not be enough space to breathe and not enough food to eat.

We are in the middle of nothing. If you disagree.

Answer these questions:

1. Why we can't stay on this Planet?
2. Why must we die?
3. What are we living for?
4. Why were we given Life?

Every living thing must die.

Could it be that we don't have enough energy within us to keep us alive for eternity?

It seems that when we die, all we had was a:

1. Body
2. Memory

So, our memory is the only thing that represented our time on this Planet.

The conclusion of life = "We all shall die"

Lesson #45 Living Involves Suffering

Life is not going to happen the way we want it too.

Everything we do is an installment of our death.

Each day we must breathe for 24 hours without stopping, even when we are sleep.

We use every square inch of this life to survive.

We are born, and then we die.

So, life is just like a cage, we live in it until we die.

The truth is that we all die little by little each day, trying to live.

I'm about to shock you again!

1. "The purpose of life is to die."
2. "We are born into a prison for our mind."

We must do the best we can do until we die.

We must put in several good and bad hours each day of our lives before it is all over.

Facts:

Adults are less alive than children.

Our bodies are factories that cannot function forever. The reason why we can't live forever is that we don't know how to deal with the energy that keeps us alive. If we knew what the energy was made of, we would be able to renew it before it dies out.

Pain & Suffering

1. Pain is a response to something wrong with you inside or outside; it's a reminder of there being a problem with you.

2. Suffering:
    - Pain
    - Distress
    - Injury
    - Loss
    - Anything unpleasant

The most significant pain is when people use you, then throw you away.

People abuse the love you have for them until you don't have any more respect for them.

Needs:

If there is a Creator. The Creator designed us with a need to eat, sleep and think.

We must spend our whole lives taking care of our needs.

So, life must be about caring for our needs.

Things we need:

1. Sleep
2. Food
3. Water
4. Air
5. Affection
6. Orgasms

What we need more than all of these is answers to what are we here on this Planet for.

"We didn't ask for our needs."

"We were just born with our needs."

The question is:

Who caused us to be put into this prison called "Life"?

The sad part is that we only can choose from what we have learned.

To live this life, our energy needs problems.

Problems come about when we:

1. Protect the liberty of what we have.
2. Protect the data we have gathered (knowledge) all our lives.
3. Protect what matters most to us.
4. Let things and people hurt us.
5. Defend our honor.

So, life is just a cage, and anything could happen to us all at any given time.

Suffering:

We get most of our suffering from people who:

1. Betray us
2. Break their promises
3. Hurt us
4. Lie to us

The biggest suffering is to protect our real identities from people that will try to rob it.

The second biggest suffering is that our thoughts can make us sick.

The third biggest suffering is that we want to know more things, then it concerns our survival.

The Fourth biggest suffering is depending on other people to help us, and they don't.

Lesson #46 Life Control

We were all taught the rules of how to live. And how to fit in with life from the people that were here before us.

Each person that is born becomes a soldier to help us build this place we call "Life" for the next generations to come.

Between the beginning of humans and now is "Progress."

Progress is the energy we all gave to this "Life."

Everything aside from the Earth and its materials come from the human mind.

What we think in our minds is more real then what is around us.

Whatever we believe becomes reality.

But, to function, we need hopes & dreams to have something to do.

On our way to doing things, we meet trouble, and trouble makes it hard for us to accomplish our hopes and dreams.

The truth is that we all spend most of our time on our hopes and dreams.

Our life is an explanation of our hopes and dreams.

Us:

1. We are made of opinions.
2. We have built a belief system for ourselves.
3. We keep our memories of our life with us until we die.

Sadly, we can live our lives to we die, and still haven't figure out who we truly are.

Society:

1. Programs us
2. Teaches us
3. Controls us
4. Lies to us
5. Hurts us
6. Betrays us
7. Confuse us
8. Withdraws us from life

These things are the only ways to control us. It teaches us to go against ourselves and to doubt ourselves. Once we assign doubt to ourselves, it means we don't trust ourselves.

Energy:

We all have energy and our energy needs problems to stay alive.

We also need problems to keep thinking.

Everything needs energy to work.

Trying:

"Trying" takes all our energy each day.

Believe it or not, we are all fucked up from "trying."

The most common "trying" is trying to be honest.

Honest:

1. Honest is staying in line while waiting to get what you want.
2. Dishonest is not waiting in line, its skipping everyone that's in the line to get ahead.

Dishonest is associated with:

1. Cheating
2. Stealing
3. Lying

All of these are for us to get what we want without earning it.

Question:

Do we suppose to try to advance whatever way we can to meet our needs, or do we suppose to stay in line to get it later and realize that we are going to die "Trying"?

Cheating, Stealing and Lying:

Cheating, Stealing and Lying only speeds up the process, so we can get to where we want to get to quick enough to enjoy it.

Question:

Is cheating, stealing, and lying a bad thing or good thing?

I believe it is using your imagination to get what you want.

If you don't pay your taxes, you are "Cheating."

If you don't pay your bills you are "Stealing."

Believe it or not, "Lying" is a gift. Because, if you lie, you are only hiding the truth.

So, if you tell the truth all the time, you will be controlled because you are not a threat to Society.

Cheaters, Thieves, and Liars are a threat to our Society.

Lesson #47 The Soul

Everyone has a soul, and the soul can get into a body and command it and tell it what to do. (Control)

That control is the first sign of us getting what we want.

While we are in a chosen body. The soul gives the body the ability to ride things like:

1. Cars
2. Bikes
3. Shoes
4. Computers
5. Cell phones
6. Pens
7. Spoons and forks
8. Machines
9. Musical instruments
10. People thoughts

The mind is not the soul.

The mind is just an information system servicing the soul.

Everything there is on earth is designed to service the soul.

The mind only records all the information it sees and hears and stores it in the brain.

So, the soul is who we are.

"I believe":

Our soul was made and manufactured somewhere before we existed. Our bodies were created by our mother and father from a universal template to house our soul to experience physical life.

There is an argument:

1. Is the soul separate from the body and comes from the Creator, and when the body dies, it returns to the Creator? (or)
2. Is the soul part of the body and dies when the body dies?

We will never know while we have life.

There are only three ways the soul can go at death; either it will die with the body, go back to where it came from and wait for instructions or journey to another reality.

Release – Answer

www.releaseanswer.com

Lesson #48 The Creator

We were created by something that has a greater purpose than our Planet and ourselves.

Our existence was well thought out before we existed.

Someone or something that has a more powerful intelligence has created us.

We were made from a material that we cannot explain.

There's an argument:

What's more important the "Creator" or "Life"?

Answer:

1. If there is life after death, the Creator is more important.
2. If there is no life after death, life is more important.

If we are supposed to be doing something after this life, what is it?

What are we here for?

1. Are we here for the experience?
2. Are we here to be tortured?

It doesn't add up; it makes no sense.

If we were created, we had to be an idea at one time, and it had to take a lot of thinking to create us and all that we see around us.

What was the reason for us being a part of life and existence?

Why were we a part of this life?

Religion has nothing to do with the Creator. Religion is only an organized thought of the Creator.

There is no way to investigate religion to prove it is true; all we have is books that were written by humans.

To know if there is more than life after death, we will have to die to find out.

Release – Answer

www.releaseanswer.com

Lesson #49 Heaven & Hell

Heaven & Hell is just a mental image.

Heaven & Hell is imagination created by religion to keep people under control in society.

Heaven & Hell:

1. Heaven represents good, love, peace, happiness, freedom, help, joy and success.
2. Hell represents evil, bad, sad, angry, stress, and death.

It is only a form of control.

It represents that doing good gets you to heaven and doing evil takes you to hell.

It means that doing good should be more important than the idea of going to hell.

Heaven & Hell are places we created with our imagination.

We created Heaven & Hell to make people fear.

The truth is that life, time, truth, lies, good, bad, and heaven & hell are all just imagination created by us.

We cannot escape death, and no one knows what will happen to them after death.

Heaven & Hell is only a theory that many humans believe in.

Heaven & Hell is only an established thought that we live by.

How most humans think:

They think that GOD is an accountant, and he measures all the good and evil we have done in this life and takes his calculator out and figures out how much sin we did and how much punishment its worth.

I believe that we produce Heaven & Hell within ourselves.

Were we in another life before this life, and put here for our sins, to get another chance to do better?

Unfortunately, I can't tell you what's real nor what's not real. All I can tell you is that we all are playing with our own "Lives."

Release – Answer

www.releaseanswer.com

Lesson #50 Decisions

Life is more than who we are. But unfortunately, we will die with the decisions we have made for ourselves. When we were living, we had to make decisions from what was available to us.

Our decisions came from our thoughts and beliefs.

We must go through a lot of thinking to get to our choices.

To make a decision, we need information. Information is the energy and fire that makes the mind work.

The information we receive here on Earth should be utilized to help ourselves.

We use information for good and evil. We have the option to choose which way to use it. When we choose what we want to do with the information, it becomes a decision.

In this life everybody wants what they see and hear; they also want what is inside of their mind.

We all want everything with no installments attached.

We all live on the level of trying to be better than someone else.

We measure ourselves against other people.

Some of us live for:

1. The joy of other people failures.
2. The joy of other people Suffering.

Joy, Love, and Peace, is hard to obtain because all we do is experience:

1. Worries
2. Distractions
3. Thinking of the past
4. Thinking of the future

To receive Joy, Love, and Peace, we must first know that we have three brains:

1. In the head = the seat of logic and intelligence. It directs 80% of our behaviors.
2. The Gut = 90% of our body's serotonin, involved in mood and management.
3. The Heart = more neural pathways are running from the heart to the head brain than from the head brain to the heart.

All brains must be aligned and in tune with each other to receive information and messages.

1. When something is wrong, we can feel it in our stomach.
2. When we love someone or something, we feel it in our heart.
3. When we think about something, we use our brain.

Facts:

1. Stress is when the three brains are not aligned.
2. Emotions are thinking in the past.
3. Responsibility is the ability to respond in the moment of need.
4. Truth is backed up by facts.
5. The eye investigates and brings about truth from proven facts.
6. Time and space are just an idea.
7. Death can't live.
8. The present time only last a second.
9. The future is the next now.
10. The body needs food and sleep.
11. When we lose trust, love withdraws.

Everybody wants to know everything about life. But, to know everything about life, everything that exists would have to slow down real slow to our intelligence, so we can acknowledge it and experience what it is to understand it.

To know all things, we must know:

1. All things are an instrument.
2. Everything is about remembering.
3. Everything we do is for a purpose.
4. Your time is someone else's future.
5. School only gives us skills to survive.
6. We only use materials and objects to create things.
7. We can think greater than we feel.
8. We will always be afraid until we know what we are doing.
9. Our body cannot live without our mind.
10. Everything we don't know leads us to believe.

All we are doing as humans are listening to what other people think. What they feel is from they believe. But they will never know what is real until they see the truth for themselves. So, everything is hearsay until it is proven to be true.

We are only living off the thoughts and beliefs of other people that came here to this life before us. Believe it or not, we have been here on this Planet for 1000's of years, and we still don't have any explanation of what all this life shit is about. All we can do is live and die for now.

Now listen very carefully.

To make better decisions, you must:

1. Get control of your time.
2. Don't pretend that you don't see something or know something that you really know.
3. If you are not satisfied with the person you are, you must change immediately.
4. Decide what you want to be and do it.
5. Stay away from people that don't service you.
6. Have your mind work for you.
7. Program yourself to be "great."
8. Don't betray, lie or hurt yourself.
9. Don't let yourself get over on you, put "you" in charge at all times, even when you sleep.
10. You don't need to be accepted by others.
11. Keep all the promises that you make to yourself.

When you put these things into order, you will be making better decisions for yourself.

Lesson #51 People & Yourself

We must get guarantees out of people until we can't get guarantees out of them anymore.

We must get guarantees while we can get it, and when people don't want to give us guarantees anymore, we must move on because guarantees are temporary.

We get emotional when people play games with our emotions.

People can:

1. Betray us
2. Break promises
3. Hurt us
4. Lie to us

The sad part is that we assign and attach our feelings to each situation.

To protect ourselves from people, we must:

1. Look at the quality of people souls to know what we are about to get into.
2. Watch out for people who want to take our attention from us, they will try to cut us off from what we must accomplish for ourselves

People have pains and problems that they will push on us.

Relationships:

1. A bad woman is a woman that doesn't want to serve you any peace.
2. A bad man is a man that wishes you harm.

If you are looking for happiness, you need someone with a friendly soul.

Yourself:

If you be nice all the time, you are going to end up used up and never getting what you want.

You would end up giving everyone around you what you needed and wanted.

The key to self is to not let yourself get over on you. You must stop kissing your own ass and stop forgiving yourself and make yourself service you.

You must determine what you want to be before you can be anything. You must want what you are going to be before you can make anything happen.

You are the driver of all the things you do.

What you know now is all you know for now.

Imagine that you went a different way with your life.

1. You wouldn't know all the things you know now.
2. You would be a different person.
3. You would know other things that you never knew before.

Understanding depends on where you have been and where you are now.

"That's called experience."

Happiness:

- Being passionate about our life.
- Having stable circumstances in our life.
- Having close and quality relationships with others in our life.

True happiness is "peace."

True happiness begins with:

1. Understanding yourself
2. Accepting yourself
3. Having confidence in yourself

It all comes down to; we all have our own smiles and cries that only belong to ourselves.

Our inner peace can only be destroyed if we keep allowing people to borrow our inner self.

Lesson #52 Trust

If you don't trust someone, your mind will have doubts about them.

Doubts are having a conversation with your mind about something that doesn't seem correct.

If you assign a doubt to someone, it means that you don't trust them.

When you lose trust in a person, the love you have for them will withdraw immediately.

Non-trust = you believed in something or someone, and the outcome was different then you expected.

When you judge something or someone, it means that you don't trust it or them.

But, when you feel the trust of something or someone, you will trust it or them.

The biggest trust in life is money, because:

1. It takes care of our needs.
2. It buys us food.
3. It buys us clothes.
4. It buys us cars.
5. It buys us entertainment.
6. It buys us education.
7. It buys us pleasure.
8. It buys us comfort.
9. It buys us better health.
10. It buys us privacy.
11. It gives us a better life.
12. It gives us confidence.
13. It gives us peace of mind.
14. It gives us security.
15. It gives us freedom.
16. It helps us get more money.

These days money = "Trust."

Release – Answer

www.releaseanswer.com

Lesson #53 The Meaning of Life

To exist, you must have space, and everything on Earth occupies space, including us.

We are a soul that only knows what it's like to be ourselves.

We are all born and developed with a body to observe what it is to be physical.

The goal is to survive as a physical person.

We are all given a period to live, roughly about 150 years, to observe what it is like to be physical.

After this experiment, our body dies, and our soul goes back to where the Creator wants it to travel. If this is not true, I would say that maybe the soul dies with the body.

It's not known if we only experience life once; perhaps we get more than one chance to experience life through different bodies.

It's also possible that we can keep repeating our life repeatedly.

Human thinks that the Earth is ours, but the truth is that the earth does not belong to us.

Because if all humankind dies, it will still be an Earth. So, there's no man without Earth.

Earth is a place we don't belong, but for some strange reason, we all ended up here.

We don't belong here because if we did, we would have been designed to never die.

Earth is only a place to learn and observe.

Earth is a place of existence for people with imagination. It's a place for souls to experience and feel what it is like to be physical.

The only way to experience the Earth, you must be in the physical.

It is believed that our soul cannot be conscious without a body on Earth.

People believe:

When a man and woman create a baby, there are souls in line waiting to be assigned to create that baby.

I Believe:

There is a most high Creator, above other creators who created us, and whoever created us was assigned to develop us from a blueprint from the highest Creator. I believe that there was a system for us to follow, but as time went on, the system was disobeyed by us.

The truth is that man will never know the truth of all things until the soul goes back to where it came from.

The soul needs to know:

1. Where it came from
2. Where it's been
3. Where it's going
4. Where it's at

Life on Earth:

Human is born to life on Earth:

We are all born into a program of life to see if we can survive under the conditions of Earth.

The goal in life is to figure out the reason we are living, and why do we die.

We are all born into a prison for our souls, "Earth."

Earth is a prison, and we are all prisoners of the Earth.

On Earth, all we do is keep our minds stimulated with all the things that we have forced ourselves to believe in so that we won't think about death. We have created religion and money to takes our minds away from dying.

We have created:

1. Time to capture sun-up and sun-down.
2. Music to be the soundtrack of our lives.
3. Religion to keep people from hurting others.
4. Language to communicate with each other.
5. Lies to deceive others.
6. Happiness to be happy.

Everyone in life will do a lot of good things and a lot of bad things. We will keep re-inventing ourselves over and over until we find a better us. Each situation we go through turns us into a different person. Because it will always be a different situation to deal with, with each situation, we will learn something from it until we have solved it completely.

Our lives:

The thought of our lives is from what we all created together as people.

We are all living through what we have created for ourselves, and that is the only thoughts we know at this time until the next generations come into this life and help us create more.

We made this life our own system:

What we put into our system determines what we will be as we progress into the future.

So, if we are made of good stuff, we will be good. But if we are made of bad things, we will be bad.

Now you know where good and bad come from.

We can only create with the things that are available to us on Earth.

In this Life:

1. We will meet people
2. We will lose people
3. We will love people
4. We will hate people
5. We will hurt people
6. We will communicate with people

In this Life:

1. People will make us happy
2. People will make us sad
3. People will make us angry
4. People will hurt us
5. People will love us
6. People will hate us

We must live with people; we have no choice at all.

The biggest question of all times is:

"Do our life experiences become helpful or useless when we die"?

I believe that when we die, we would no longer need our life experiences.

But, if for some special reason our life experiences are needed, it would only mean that there is life after death.

But, if we all died and there is no afterlife, it would mean that there is not enough life to keep all of us alive.

The truth is that if it is no life after death, we were all mind Fucked!

The Bottom line, we can believe whatever we want to believe, but the truth to everything is way beyond our thinking and understanding…

Release – Answer

www.releaseanswer.com

ACKNOWLEDGMENTS

This book would not have been possible without the support and encouragement of my family and friends.

First, I would like to thank my aunt Millie Fulford for teaching me how to write. Aunt Millie came to the rescue for me when I needed her the most in my life. I love her. She didn't even charge me money.

I want to thank my children, Shakoiya S. Flagg and Stephen E. Flagg, which is my extra "Memory" in Life.

I want to thank my sister Kimberly S. Flagg

I want to thank my three best friends:

1. Russell Pressley
2. Timothy Patterson
3. Lawrence Joseph

I want to thank my cousin Tyrone "Fly-ty" Williams, President of Cold Chillin Records, for giving me a record deal in 1994; he came through for me when I needed him.

I want to thank John "Mook" Gibbons, President of Wu-tang Management, for allowing me to work with him in 1998; he came through for me when I needed him.

I want to thank Noah Katz, President of PSK Supermarkets, Food town, New York, for being my friend for over 30 years. He taught me to work hard, and he watched me grow.

I want to thank Marques Robinson my graphics guy.

I want to thank my Assistant Shimika Finney.

I want to thank the Staff of Port Richmond Public Library of Staten Island, New York 1997 to 1999 for allowing me to read every book on the self.
75 Bennett Street, Staten Island, NY 10302

I want to thank the Staff of Brooklyn New York Supreme Court Law Library of Kings County 1992 to 1999 for allowing me to read every law book on the shelf.
360 Adams Street, room 349, Brooklyn, NY 11201

I want to thank the Staff of SUNY Downstate Health Science University 1995-1998 for allowing me to read every book on the self.
450 Clarkson Ave, Brooklyn, NY 11203

I want to thank the Students of New York University of New York (dome room) 2001 for coming downstairs to teach me Law while I was an overnight security officer.
63 Greenwich Street. New York, NY 10014

I want to thank the State of New York and New Jersey for allowing me to serve as a Police Officer in both States. Which allowed me to obtain my Security Watch Guard Agency.

I want to thank Vernon Earl "The Pearl" Monroe former New York Knicks basketball Team player for giving me a record deal on Pretty Pearl Records in 1986.

IN MEMORY

My Mother Geraldine Fulford Flagg

My Father Joseph Flagg II

My Brother Joseph Flagg III

My Grandfather Joseph Flagg I

My Grandfather Freddie Fulford

My Grandmother Lula May Flagg

My Grandmother Mildred Fulford

My Cousin Emery Flagg Gardner

My Cousin Eric Flagg Gardner

My Aunt Matty Fulford

My Aunt Carol Samms

My Aunt Sharon Ellis

My Aunt Cora Flagg

My Best Friend Jason Solomon

Mr. Magic WBLS

My Cat Gucci

Release - Answer

www.releaseanswer.com

Release Answer

An Incredible new Website designed to answer any question.

Release - Answer is comprised of a group of geniuses that can answer any and every question a person can ask for absolutely free. If we don't know the answer, we will research your question more in-depth and provide you with the best answer. No questions go unanswered at "Release – Answer."

The process is very easy !!! Just simply type in an email address, then type in a question, then click the submit button. Release – Answer will then deliver an answer to your question as soon as possible.

To answer every question, "Release – Answer" has an incredible team of specialists. Teachers, Professors, Scientists, Accountants, Financial Advisers, Bankers, Lawyers, Judges, Government Officials, Doctors, Builders, Reverends, Architects, Detectives, etc.

There are thousands of questions that knock the walls of our brains every day, which leaves us with a great deal of unanswered questions that demands the true answer to tackle our problems. "Release – Answer" will research your question and find the answer for you for free. Life, for the most part, is full of mysteries, but, with Release – Answer you will get your questions answered. "There will be no questions unanswered," we put our name on the line.

"Release – Answer" is proud to be the Website to solve the World's most complex questions.

To get your questions answered, please visit the "Release – Answer" Website at:

www.releaseanswer.com

www.ingramcontent.com/pod-product-compliance
Lightning Source LLC
Chambersburg PA
CBHW021229090426
42740CB00006B/454